The body, culture and society

The body, culture and society

AN INTRODUCTION

PHILIP HANCOCK
BILL HUGHES
ELIZABETH JAGGER
KEVIN PATERSON
RACHEL RUSSELL
EMMANUELLE TULLE-WINTON
MELISSA TYLER

Open University Press
Buckingham · Philadelphia

Open University Press
Celtic Court
22 Ballmoor
Buckingham
MK18 1XW

email: enquiries@openup.co.uk
world wide web: www.openup.co.uk

and
325 Chestnut Street
Philadelphia, PA 19106, USA

First Published 2000

A catalogue record of this book is available from the British Library

ISBN   0 335 20413 9 (pb)   0 335 20414 7 (hb)

Library of Congress Cataloging-in-Publication Data
The body, culture, and society: an introduction / Philip Hancock . . . [et al.].
    p. cm.
  Includes bibliographical references and index.
  ISBN 0–335–20414–7 — ISBN 0–335–20413–9 (pbk.)
  1. Body, Human—Social aspects. 2. Body image. 3. Sociology of
disability. 4. Aging. 5. Social ethics. 6. Medical ethics. I. Hancock,
Philip, 1965– .

HM636.B6 2000
306.4—dc21   00–037446

Typeset by Graphicraft Limited, Hong Kong
Printed in Great Britain by Biddles Ltd, Guildford and King's Lynn

For Alan

Contents

Notes on contributing authors

Philip Hancock has taught the sociology of work and organizations at several UK universities. He is a member of the Caledonian University Body and Social Theory research group and an associate member of the Centre for Social Theory and Technology at Keele University. He has published in a number of edited collections, as well as in journals such as *Organization* and *The Journal of Management Studies*.

Bill Hughes is Head of Division of Sociology at Glasgow Caledonian University. His teaching responsibilities are concentrated primarily in the areas of the body, health and social theory. He is a member of the Caledonian University Body and Social Theory research group and his current research focuses on the application of contemporary socio-logical theory to impairment and disability. He has published in *Body & Society* and *Disability & Society*.

Elizabeth Jagger is a lecturer in sociology at Glasgow Caledonian University and Chair of the Body and Social Theory research group. Her teaching and research interests are the body, consumption and mass media and popular culture. She has published on professional and governmental responses to glue-sniffing in several leading policy journals and, more recently, work from her ongoing research into dating has appeared in *Sociology*.

Kevin Paterson is a research student in the School of Social Sciences at Glasgow Caledonian University. His research and teaching focuses on disability studies and the body. He is interested in the development of a sociology of impairment and has had several articles published on this subject in edited collections and the journal *Disability & Society*.

Rachel Russell lectures in philosophy and the sociology of culture at Glasgow Caledonian University. Her research and publishing activities have recently focused on the interface between ethics and aesthetic experience, and its implication for social theory. She is a member of the Caledonian University Body and Social Theory research group and is Coordinator of the Division of Sociology Research Seminar Series.

Emmanuelle Tulle-Winton teaches in the field of old age and health at Glasgow Caledonian University and is a member of the Caledonian University Body and Social Theory research group. She has conducted research and published in a number of edited collections and journals on issues around the government of old age and old bodies as well as the organizational features of mental health services.

Melissa Tyler teaches gender and feminist theory, work and organization studies and mass media and popular culture at Glasgow Caledonian University. She is a member of the Caledonian University Body and Social Theory research group and has published in various edited collections and journals on issues of gender, aesthetics, organization and the body.

Acknowledgements

We would like to extend our thanks to colleagues and students at Glasgow Caledonian University who have engaged with our emergent ideas and contributed to their clarification. We are also grateful to all the reviewers for their contribution to this process. Specifically we would like to single out Chris Shilling for his helpful and supportive comments on the finished manuscript, as well as Pamela Abbott, Martin Parker and Mike Hepworth for constructive and insightful feedback at various stages in the production of this book.

Introduction

By the close of the twentieth century the body had become a key site of political, social, cultural and economic intervention in relation, for example, to medicine, disability, work, consumption, old age and ethics. In short, the body has come to be recognized as a contested terrain on which struggles over control and resistance are fought out in contemporary societies. That the body has emerged in recent years as a key problematic in the social sciences is indicated, for instance, by the proliferation of books and journals, conferences and other media dedicated to a sociological analysis of the body. Similarly, courses on the body and related issues feature increasingly in undergraduate and postgraduate programmes. In contemporary societies body issues are everywhere. For example, new social movements struggle for citizenship and emancipation in the name of excluded bodies (Nicholson and Seidman 1995). There has been a radical shift in the understanding of disability and old age from a medical and welfare perspective to a focus on embodiment as a human rights issue. Ethics are fought out at the level of aesthetics and relations between bodies. Projects of self-enhancement and bodily transformation are the focus of embodiment as a consumer lifestyle. Medicine is shifting its focus from diseased to healthy bodies. Transnational capitalism demands flexible bodies for flexible accumulation and the organization of the body on an unprecedented scale.

These particular developments, which spell out the presence of the body in social, moral and political life, have had a profound impact on sociology and social theory and for this reason form the basic themes of this book. The assumption of classical positivist sociology, that bodies belong primarily to biology, has collapsed and the meaning of the body has become a problem for linguistic, cultural and social analysis. This inclusion of the body in sociological inquiry can be regarded as a critical and reflective response to the social changes which have brought the body to the forefront of contemporary struggle and debate. Its intellectual roots are diverse, although poststructuralism and feminism can claim to be at its core; and Nietzsche and the critique of Cartesian dualism, important in phenomenological thought, are its most notable theoretical ancestors. Like the world it seeks to describe and explain, the sociology of the body is a place of twists and turns, uncertainties and ambiguities, a place where the long, unchallenged reign of reason is in dispute. In epistemology, sociological inquiry into the body tends to opt for pragmatism; in methodology it embraces pluralism; in ontology it tends to try to escape the traps of essentialism and foundationalism. Debates in feminism and the 'philosophy of difference' have been key players in shaping the intellectual hue of the sociology of the body. Yet the arrival of this new subdiscipline in sociology is not simply a response to the theoretical pluralism and the cross-fertilization of disciplines that have collapsed the boundaries between the human sciences in the contemporary world. We feel that it is necessary to say a little about the social and cultural events that have provoked the claim that we live in a 'somatic society' (Turner 1996: 1) – that is, a society 'within which major political and personal problems are both problematized within the body and expressed through it'.

Flexible bodies

In summing up *The Dialectic of Enlightenment* and exposing the key value of modernity, Horkheimer and Adorno wrote: 'What men want to learn from nature is how to use it in order to wholly dominate it and other men. That is the only aim' (1973: 28). Although one might contest this singular and absolute account of modern times, it does suggest a re-ordering of the relationship between culture and nature in which the former acquires a privileged status. Nature, including the body, has become something to be commanded and disciplined. Over the past 300 years the planetary body has been subjected to human exploitation on a massive scale, and human embodiment, emotions and desires have been 'civilized' by the coincidental rise of the modern state and the proliferation of formal modes of conduct (Elias 1978). For Foucault (1971: 153) the body is moulded by 'a great many distinct regimes'. It is an outcome of the play of power, and power 'reaches into the very grain of individuals, touches their bodies and inserts itself into their actions and attitudes, their discourses, learning processes and everyday lives' (Foucault 1978: 39). The heady combination of feminism and poststructuralism has produced the claim that not only gender but sex is a social construction (see, for example, Butler 1993), and Haraway (1990) has argued that the ubiquitous couplings of flesh and machine that we witness in contemporary times are evidence of the rise of cyborg culture.

Underpinning this widespread cultural agenda of the body at the end of the twentieth century is a powerful emphasis on its malleability. 'We have become responsible for the design of our own bodies' (Giddens 1991: 102). No longer is the body conceived as a fixed essence. The changes that it undergoes are no longer regarded as wholly dependent on natural physiological processes. As the celebrity Cher once put it: 'Nature isn't always the best. I have the money to improve on nature and I don't see why I shouldn't' (*Glasgow Evening Times*, 24 April 1992). The boundaries between culture and nature have collapsed and the body has become flexible: 'Flexibility is an object of desire for nearly everyone's personality, body and organisation' (Martin 1994: xvii). The body has become plastic, a lifestyle accessory, a thing to be sculpted, shaped and 'stylized' (Featherstone 1991a). It has been transformed from a biological fact into a 'project' (Giddens 1991) and a 'performance' (Goffman 1971b). Contemporary culture is marked by a quest for physiognomical and physical regimes of embodiment that are based on the assumption that the surface and the interior of the body are amenable to reconstruction or re-incorporation. As Anthony Giddens (1991: 7–8) has argued: 'The reflexivity of self in conjunction with abstract systems pervasively affects the body [. . .] The body is less and less an extrinsic given functioning outside the internally referential systems of modernity, but becomes itself reflexively mobilised.'

These claims, which transform our ideas about the body from obdurate matter to flexible performance, have powerful empirical points of reference in popular culture and new technologies. The organ transplant trade raises questions not only about the ownership of the body but also about its boundaries (Elshtian and Cloyd 1995). The notion that nature constitutes an absolute limitation is an idea in decline. The body conceived as a project opens up possibilities for its re-formation and modification. 'Body work' is no longer simply a question of mechanical maintenance but one of lifestyle choice and identity. Shaping the body through diet, exercise and cosmetic surgery is a fleshy testimonial to the aestheticization of everyday life (Featherstone 1992; Welsch 1996), a fascination with appearance and, some argue, the narcissism of contemporary culture (Lasch 1980).

The fitness, health and dieting booms of the 1970s and 1980s supported the marketing of all sorts of commodities and techniques for bodily enhancement. For a significant number of women dieting can take on vocational proportions and one study claims that only 10 per cent of women have never dieted (Ogden 1992). Health farms and fat farms sell dreams of the body beautiful and offer a range of techniques and therapies for shaping body and soul. In the USA Weight Watchers claims a membership of eight million whereas those who want to go it alone can choose from hundreds of best-selling slimming books, exercise videos, machines or classes or can pick up any popular magazine and read about the thousands of food items, concoctions, exercise regimes, body-building programmes and pharmaceuticals that claim to help in the battle against the unfashionable body. For those who can afford it, there is the option of the surgeon's knife, used widely in the West to combat the ageing process, to eliminate unwanted physical features (K. Davis 1995) or even as a means of mobilizing the body as an artistic canvas (K. Davis 1997b).

The possibilities for self-transformation have extended to sexual identity. Once regarded as fixed and impervious to modification, sexual identity has been relocated from the kingdom of necessity to the land of choice. Today, 'normal sexuality is simply one type of lifestyle choice among others' (Giddens 1992: 179). In light of the growth and recognition of 'diverse sexual proclivities' the discourse of perversion has collapsed (Giddens 1992: 179). With improvements in reproductive and 'sex change' technology and the arrival of artificially produced conception, 'sexuality is at last fully autonomous' (Giddens 1992: 27) and sexuality has become 'plastic'. The proliferation of projects of self-identity that involve new ways of being in the body and expressing its sexuality mean that in the age of 'plastic sexuality' gender identity is no longer embedded in a fixed biological foundation. Anything goes: sex too is a reflexive project.

Sociological bodies

Now that the body itself is mobilized in the name of a host of practices and projects of self-transformation, there has been a simultaneous proliferation of sociological bodies. These bodies have been predominantly a) theoretical, b) historical or c) analytical – or, more accurately, theory, history or heuristic devices, including matrixes and taxonomies, have been used as the basis for distinguishing between types of body and embodiment.

(a) The highly contested domain of sociological theory provides an interesting playground in which perspectives tussle with one another over which is the more efficacious in relation to interpreting and understanding embodiment. Chris Shilling (1993) provides an excellent guide to social and sociological theories of the body and Bryan S. Turner (1996) weaves insightful essays on bodies by pragmatically threading together a variety of theories, most notably poststructuralism (especially the work of Michel Foucault), phenomenology and feminism.

(b) Feher, Naddaff and Tazi (1989) have argued that across time, the cultural nuances of embodiment can be traced in terms of a continuum between the deified, godlike body on the one hand, and the body conceived as machine or animal on the other. In their engaging study of the relationship between community and embodiment, in which the ambiguity of the corporeal is a consequence of its struggle between sensuality and rationality, Mellor and Shilling (1997) refer to medieval, protestant modern and baroque bodies.

(c) Of the various attempts to develop an analytical framework for the sociology of the body, the two most celebrated and coherent are associated with the work of Turner (1996) and Frank (1991). Turner focuses on the tasks that society sets itself in relation to the 'government of the body'. These tasks are reproduction, restraint, regulation and representation. Individual bodies (internally and externally) and populations (across space and time) are regulated in terms of these basic tasks, which every society must confront. The form of government of the body can vary depending on the institutional means used to implement the tasks. Asceticism, patriarchy, panopticism and commodification constitute the range of possible means. Frank's typology of sociological bodies is derived partly from a critical reflection on Turner's work. He displaces the functionalist flavour of Turner's typology with a framework that is indebted to the North American tradition of 'symbolic interactionism', where the emphasis is on agency and active bodies rather than bodies which are heavily informed by institutional and structural constraints. Frank offers a 'typology of body use in action' in which disciplined, dominating, mirroring and communicative bodies are the key terms in the analytical framework (Frank 1991: 54).

These two analytical approaches produce body types that are theoretically grounded and synthetic. This text is not so bold. Our ambition is accessibility and to this end we aim to provide a prequel to the complexities of theoretical and analytical synthesis and a salient review of some of the literature that opens up and smooths over the gap between the sociology of the body and (some) other sociological subdisciplines. Our typology is, therefore, nearer to the one offered by Frank in a review essay of 1990, in which he divided his material into medicalized, sexual, disciplined and talking bodies. We too have adopted substantive categories which are not dependent on or constrained by fidelity to a single theoretical framework. In so doing we have followed our own interests and specialisms in old age, ethics, organization, disability, medicine and consumption. All of these fields of investigation can be regarded (arguably) as sociological subdisciplines and we have attempted to trace the impact of the sociology of the body in these specific domains. Our terrain, therefore, is an intellectually fertile one in which new ideas and perspectives have helped to revivify more established bodies of knowledge. We do not claim to have left no stone unturned. There are other bodies – religious, sporting, sexual, emotional, knowing, for example – that are equally amenable to this treatment, but these are beyond the scope of this book.

The bodies that we have selected for discussion arise in the domain of contested modernity in which the case for pleasure, desire, sensuality and emotion challenges the rather jaded Enlightenment values of reason, truth and progress. It is this broad context which forces embodiment on to the sociological agenda. Whatever prefix we use to describe modernity, it is not what it used to be, and debates about old age, ethics, organization, disability, medicine and consumption are all embedded in and reflect the precariousness of the times in which we live. We live in an 'age of anxiety' in which existential and ontological insecurity is rife (Giddens 1991), and where our faith in the grand thoughts and designs of the past has weakened (Lyotard 1984). Our time is one of irony and nihilism, fundamentalism and anti-foundationalism, globalization and localization, geopolitical re-alignment and ecological crisis, postcolonialism and the decline of the nation-state, new nationalisms and the unimpeded expansion of trans-national corporations. We live – we hear – in interesting times, perhaps even apocalyptic ones, in which the values of the past seem both remote and ripe for review. The body and embodiment have figured strongly in this ongoing re-evaluation of values, largely because reason has come to be regarded as a false god. Modernity in its aged and uncertain state has become nostalgic for the mythical, baroque, fleshy energy of its youth.

Modern bodies

The dominant representation of the body in modernity has been provided by the biomedical discourse which became, in the nineteenth century, a science of universal bodily processes. However, in Chapter 1 – 'Medicalized bodies' – Bill Hughes argues that biomedicine now seems to be in a crisis of legitimization, and alternative, more holistic concepts of medicine and embodiment are challenging its hegemony. Biomedicine has come under fire from epidemiologists, social scientists, feminists, gay and disabled people, theologians and – most tellingly – lay persons. In an attempt to incorporate these critiques and to respond to changes in the nature of disease as well as the economic imperatives of neoliberalism, medicine is repositioning itself as a biopsychosocial practice (Armstrong 1987) in which health maintenance – rather than disease (and its) elimination – is becoming the locus for health-care organization and intervention. The chapter focuses on the ways in which medicine is transforming its conception of the body from a passive receptacle of disease to a responsible and active agent of self-care. Contemporary medicine prescribes and dispenses not only pharmaceuticals, but also information and advice about how to live, and its notion of what constitutes health work has expanded beyond clinical action to include lay vigilance in relation to behaviour, lifestyle, patterns of consumption and the organization of social space.

The medicalization of disability in the nineteenth century marked the 'scientific' exclusion of disabled people from the mainstream of social life. It is only since the emergence of the Disability Movement – sometimes described as 'the last civil rights movement' – that the experience of disability has been evaluated from a non-medical perspective. Ironically, to date, disability studies and the sociology of the body have not provided a great deal of intellectual nourishment for one another. However, disabled activists have challenged the medical model in which disability is viewed as a bodily limitation, and replaced it with a social model in which disability is defined as a situation produced by a socio-spatial environment that fails to acknowledge the needs and rights of people with impairments. This model is rooted predominantly in a structural analysis (Finkelstein 1980; Abberley 1987; Oliver 1990). It made good political sense, initially, for disability activists (like feminists) to marginalize embodied experience because biological arguments had been used historically to legitimate social exclusion. In Chapter 2 – 'Disabled bodies' – Kevin Paterson and Bill Hughes argue that a disembodied view of disability is no longer tenable. They reflect on changes in disability studies which seek an embodied view of disability and develop what has been called a social model or sociology of impairment. The chapter traces the ways in which 'the body' and 'the social' compete in the constitution of the meaning of disability.

In Chapter 3 – 'Consumer bodies' – Liz Jagger outlines the view that some of the major social transformations of modernity – including changes in work organization and techniques, the decline of heavy industry, the increasing importance of the service and leisure industries and the rise of the media and advertising – established the foundations of a consumer culture (Featherstone 1991a) and brought questions of 'self' to the front of the political, social and economic stage. Self-identity is now derived not from work and production, but from consumption (Tomlinson 1990). Moreover, with the decline of religious authority and a loss of faith in grand political narratives – two of the key markers of postmodernity – the physical body seems to provide a locus and a focus for the affirmation of identity. It provides the medium through which messages about self-identity are transmitted and is a key site for the marking of difference (Shilling 1993, 1997). The chapter explores the connections between consumption, identity and the body, drawing on the work of writers who, in diverse ways, have addressed these links. For Bourdieu (1984) consumer choices are inscribed on the body and therefore make it a site of social and especially class differences. Thus, we consume according to who we are. By contrast, for some so-called postmodern theorists we become what we consume. The body is saturated with cultural signs with no fixed referents and, as a consequence, produces multiple, shifting identities (Jameson 1985; Baudrillard 1988b). However, given that access to cultural resources for identity construction is not equally available to men and women in consumer society, reflexive self-fashioning (Giddens 1991) is more problematic for women (Lury 1997). To exemplify the contingent and uncertain nature of feminine subjectivity, Chapter 3 concludes with a discussion of a specific bodily practice that is no longer a prerogative of masculine embodiment, namely body building.

The body – built firm and strong – has become, in modernity, a sign of moral worth, and the worship of youth and beauty has made 'strangers' of older people. The moral alterity of older people is compounded by economic arguments which classify the growing elderly population as fiscal muggers who can neither produce nor reproduce. Ageism is rife and older people are regarded as the embodiment of deterioration and decay. In Chapter 4 – 'Old bodies' – Emmanuelle Tulle-Winton discusses the body as a contested site for the constitution of old age and old people. The emergence of old age as the object of professional study and practice in the late eighteenth century gave rise to a range of possible narratives about the experience of being old. The variable emphasis on and explanatory power given to the bodily manifestations of becoming and being old, and their potential for liberation, define these narratives. Chapter 4 charts these narratives, starting with the problematization of old age as a primarily medical event where the body takes centre stage. This gives rise to the modernist discourse of old age – as biological decline, physiological and mental decrepitude and loss. The constitution of old age as a biological event overdetermining the actual experience of later life was reinforced by the emergence of gerontology, the study of old age, which reflected, justified and constructed the cultural, economic and symbolic obsolescence of old people (Lynott and Lynott 1996). Its aim was to construct strategies of adaptation to loss.

There have been two principal challenges to the medicalization of old age. The first focused on the structural determinants of old age and embodied the argument that economic exclusion and discriminatory welfare practices were constitutive of the othering of old people and marked an obsession with the corporeality of the ageing body. The second was based on the cultural problematization of old bodies as posing a threat to the norm of identity which was calibrated against the valorization of youthfulness. This perspective proposed ways to manage (away) the old body and, thus, enable old people to maintain intact the integrity of their personal identity. There was, however, a cost attached to this. On the one hand, it led to the rehabilitation of successful agers, through the extension of middle age and the encouragement to keep a close check on bodily deterioration through a range of techniques of the self. On the other hand, it exacerbated the marginalization of those who could not escape old age; especially very old people or ill old people. The chapter concludes that, despite efforts to do so, old bodies cannot be abrogated and that there may be a case for attempting to recover the fleshiness of the old body without losing sight of the social and cultural processes that contribute to the marginalization of old people.

Although the bodies of post-productive people have been made anthropologically strange by the narrow moralities and economic necessities of modernity, working bodies face the disciplinarity and demands of flexibility which pervade organizations in late capitalist society. Contemporary sociological accounts of the relationship between work, its organization and the human body have been shaped by a number of recent developments both in sociology and in the world of work itself. These include, for example, shifting philosophical perspectives on the body, changes in working patterns and an increased academic and managerial concern with organizational culture. The impact of such developments has been further exacerbated by the rise of post-Fordist modes of production and exchange and the demands of an expanding tertiary sector, which has resulted in even greater attention being paid to issues of image and appearance by organizations concerned with maintaining global competitiveness. Integral to this has been the substantial increase in the proportion of jobs in which people are employed, specifically in front-line 'customer facing' service providers. It is their bodies that become the carriers of the aesthetic concerns of contemporary organization(s).

In Chapter 5 – 'Working bodies' – Philip Hancock and Melissa Tyler open with a brief discussion of these developments and their implications for the management of the body at work. They adopt a broadly historical perspective on the management and rationalization of the working body, with particular reference to the development of wage labour in western capitalist societies. Commencing with a review of these managerial systems, developed largely in the early twentieth century, which were concerned with the efficient use of the body's capacity to labour, the authors chart the refinement of various technologies of rationalization and their eventual impact on the body in contemporary work organizations. This prefigures a consideration of the significant contribution that feminist sociology has made to the understanding of the role played by the body in the management of gender differences in the workplace. The chapter ends by shifting attention away from the formal domain of paid work to focus on what Shilling (1993) has called 'body work'. This refers to the time, effort and resources dedicated to maintaining a particular state of embodiment in everyday life. The conclusion suggests that this concept offers a potentially useful way of understanding the relationship between work and the human body, one that rejects an artificial distinction between work and consumption.

If reflection on contemporary organization suggests a problem with the distinction between work and consumption, contemporary work on ethics suggests that the distinction between ethics and aesthetics is also difficult to sustain. The body is a key player in the deconstruction of this distinction. The rationale for an embodied ethics arises out of the convergence of two dominant sociological trends: the re-emergence of the moral *and* the new prominence of the body as the ethical subject in sociology. In Chapter 6 – 'Ethical bodies' – Rachel Russell discusses general processes of contemporary moralization and examines the conceptualization of the body as a site for the embodiment of ethics in two ways. First, she explores 'aesthetic ethics' and considers the historical origins of the notion that 'you are what you look like' (Synnott 1993). Second, by way of a critical consideration of the emergence of ethical subjects in the realm of consumption and new social movements, she examines the ideas of Foucault (1997) and Maffesoli (1996). The emphasis on the rational and visual in these approaches (Jay 1994) is contrasted with those that privilege the emotional and sensual dimensions of embodied ethics (Levinas 1981; Bauman 1993; Irigaray 1993; Maffesoli 1996; Smart 1996). The distinction between the rational and the emotional, and the visual and the sensual is illustrated by a consideration of the way in which ethical bodies are understood in contemporary society and social theory. A comparison of these two approaches to embodied ethics suggests that alternative sociological approaches to ethical bodies can be identified. Perspectives that transcend ontological duality and allow for an understanding of the ethical subject as emerging from embodied interaction are beginning to provide the focus for scholarship and action in this area.

Concluding remarks: the somatic turn

Sociology is a subject that embraces trends. Other disciplines have rare and fundamental 'paradigm shifts' but the contested nature of sociology and its imperative to engage with social change gives its content a flexible character and a rather charming instability. In the past two decades, the sociology of the body has become fashionable. Once the sole domain of the biological sciences, bodies and embodiment have become focal points for discussions for a whole range of sociological issues, including – to name but a few – identity, social movements, consumer culture, ethics and even social theory and philosophy. Indeed, the social processes that underpin these issues have themselves been important in generating sociological debate about the body. It is a commonplace of contemporary social science discourse to speak of the linguistic and cultural turns. One might also speak of a somatic turn. Once social scientists became uncomfortable with the distinction between nature and culture, the idea of the body as a pre-social object became difficult to sustain. The impact of post-Cartesian philosophy – particularly in its phenomenological and poststructuralist guises – was such that sociologists felt compelled to interrogate the place of embodiment in social life, and a world disgruntled by rationality went in search of sensuality, pleasure and desire. Meanwhile, the body was making itself ever-present in social and political life, be it in the shape of a battered woman, a terminated fetus, a victim of torture or televised war, a proud celebration of womanhood, disability, colour or homosexuality, an organ in transit for transplantation, a human-machine stepping on the moon, a sample of DNA under the microscope, a man who was a woman or vice versa, a body transformed by diet, exercise or the surgeon's knife, a homeless person camped on the streets of the world's richest nation, a mass grave, or another world record smashed.

To engage with the somatic turn this book focuses on a series of 'typical' bodies that correspond to those substantive subject areas in which the meaning of the contemporary body (arguably) is most vigorously contested. In this respect, we have three principal objectives: first, to introduce sociological perspectives on the body, outlining and evaluating their contribution to contemporary sociology; second, to outline the various ways in which 'the body' is conceptualized in sociology and the relative importance accorded to the body in understanding society and social relations; and third, to identify key themes in theoretically distinct perspectives on the body through an examination of various substantive bodies, including medical bodies, disabled bodies, working bodies, consuming bodies, old bodies and ethical bodies. We hope that readers use the book to pitch themselves into the somatic turn and join with us in exploring its fascinating legacy.

CHAPTER 1

Medicalized bodies

BILL HUGHES

Introduction

If someone is in pain, it is not simply a matter of biology. For a start, the presence of pain has to be recognized and therefore experienced. This experience constitutes a moment in which the biological, the emotional and the social collapse into one another. 'Pain', therefore, 'needs to be reclaimed from exclusive biomedical jurisdiction and relocated at the juncture between biology and culture' (Bendelow and Williams 1995: 159). Such a claim could also be made about the body itself. It too needs to be rescued from one-sided biomedical explanations. For biomedicine, the body is defined in purely biological terms. It is pre-social and has no history. It is an essence, a timeless, material thing. It has no cultural meaning and cannot think, feel or relate to others. Such a body is 'typically assumed to be a fixed, material entity subject to the empirical rules of biological science, existing prior to the mutability and flux of cultural change and diversity and characterized by unchangeable inner necessities' (Csordas 1994: 6). Indeed, as Shildrick (1997: 214–15) argues, for biomedicine 'the body is scarcely considered at all but is taken simply as the gross material basis of health care practices'.

The biomedical body owes its birthright to Cartesian philosophy (Seymour 1998). In this guise, it is simply a child of nature. However, sociology confounds this possibility by suggesting that nature and society are not mutually exclusive categories. Categorical distinctions, in a world where all kinds of boundaries seem to be collapsing, are not popular today. Sociology is alive to this, but medicine is not.

Consequently, the bodies that people the sociological imagination are a reflection of the fragmentation of contemporary life and thought and the medical body is differentiated only on the grounds of sex.

There are significant differences between sociological bodies and the medical body. The first thing to note is that the former is plural and the latter singular (at best twofold if one distinguishes between the sexes). The body in sociology is highly contested. By contrast, in medicine it has an objective, scientific, universal, indeed 'real' status. For medicine, the reality of the body is a practical necessity. Sociology, on the other hand, can deal with all sorts of bodies, largely because it relates to them primarily as either the source or the outcome of meaning (Lloyd 1999). In the past 15 years or so, sociological bodies have proliferated. They have been defined by their 'docility' (Foucault 1977), their 'performativity' (Butler 1993) and their 'lived' carnality (Merleau-Ponty 1962; Crossley 1995; Nettleton and Watson 1998); and embodiment has been explored in terms of its government (Turner 1996), its 'physical capital' (Bourdieu 1984), its 'effervescence' (Mellor and Shilling 1997) and the impact on it of the 'civilizing process' (Elias 1978).

The influence of constructionism and postmodernism in sociology is strong whereas in medical science it is nebulous. Contemporary sociological ideas are often wrapped up in a world of ambivalence, deregulation, insecurity and uncertainty (Bauman 1991). Medicine, on the other hand, cannot survive as an effective practice without assuming that the body that it seeks to mend is a secure and orderly thing that is obedient to the laws of anatomy and physiology. One could not, for example, expect the average surgeon to pay much attention to the claim that '[a] body analysed for humours contains humours; a body analysed for organs and tissues is constituted by organs and tissues; a body analysed for psychosocial functioning is a psychosocial object' (Armstrong 1994: 25). Medical practice is a servant of positivism and common sense. Our hypothetical surgeon would be unlikely to give up the 'universal truth' of the body for Armstrong's suggestion that it might contain many contradictory truths. As a practitioner, he or she would also be bound to overlook the fact that the body is a source of desire, pleasure and passion. Whereas contemporary social thought may be keen to take note of and even focus on these unruly elements of embodied life, medicine ignores them.

Despite the general stability of the medical conception of the body, I want to argue in this chapter that it is undergoing some significant changes, not so much in content but by the way it is becoming contextualized. These changes can be summed up by two propositions. First, the medical body is changing from a passive to an active entity. Given that ordinary people – rather than medical experts – are now expected to be responsible for their own well-being, the healthy body has been redefined as flexible in character (Martin 1994). It can be mobilized, by lay people, as a resource in their biographical projects of self-identity (Giddens 1991). Second, as medicine begins to prioritize health maintenance as opposed to the elimination of disease, the body is being rethought in terms of its relationship to both lifestyle and the environment (Bunton *et al.* 1995). In other words, biomedicine has come to recognize that the body exists in a psychosocial context that is relevant to its health and well-being. These propositions can, in turn, be located analytically in the process by which medicine is being transformed from a biomedical to a biopsychosocial practice (Armstrong 1987, 1993; Cooper *et al.* 1996). It is in the lap of this transition – to a 'regime of total health' (Armstrong 1993; Nettleton 1995: 227) – that we must place ourselves if we are to understand the changing nature of the medical body.

From the biomedical to the biopsychosocial body

The dominant representation of the body in modernity has been provided by biomedical discourse. In the nineteenth century, biomedicine became a science of universal bodily processes. However, it now seems to be in crisis. Alternative, particularly more holistic, conceptions of embodiment are challenging its monopoly over the 'truth' about bodily existence. Biomedicine has come under fire from epidemiologists, social scientists, feminists, gay and disabled people, animal rights activists, alternative therapists, theologians and – most tellingly – lay persons (Gabe *et al.* 1994). In an attempt to incorporate these critiques and to respond to changes in the nature of disease, medicine seems to be repositioning itself as a biopsychosocial practice. Health maintenance, rather than disease and its elimination, is slowly becoming the focus for medical organization and intervention.

In the twentieth century medicine dominated our conception of the body. Anything that could be shown to be a concern for the body – including the big themes of life and death – was articulated in a language that if not medical per se, more often than not could be traced to it. Modern cosmopolitan medicine or biomedicine dominated the moral, political and social terrain with respect to health, illness and the body. Biomedicine can be defined as follows:

> [It] is reductionist in form, seeking explanations of dysfunctions in invariant biological structures and processes: it privileges such explanations at the expense of social, cultural and biographical explanations. In its clinical mode, this dominant model of medical reasoning implies that diseases exist as distinct entities; that these entities are revealed through the inspection of 'signs' and 'symptoms'; that the individual patient is more or less a passive site of disease manifestation; that diseases are to be understood as categorical departures from normality.
>
> (Atkinson 1988: 180)

At its simplest, the concept of biomedicine refers to modern scientific medicine. As a body of knowledge about the body (and to a lesser extent the mind) it is based on the principles of scientific observation applied principally to corpses. Through this work, it has produced and draws on the disciplines of anatomy, physiology and pathology. Biomedicine seeks knowledge of the human body in order to repair it when it goes wrong. As Engel (1977: 131) put it, biomedicine regards the 'body as a machine and . . . the doctor's task as the repair of the machine'. It is concerned, therefore, with producing a map or a picture of the normal body in order to identify and eliminate abnormality or disease. According to Foucault (1976b: 35), medicine becomes biomedicine when its scientific endeavours focus on charting the contours of normality – that is, when it becomes concerned with 'a regular functioning of the organism' and seeks to identify 'where it had deviated, what it was disturbed by and how it could be brought back into working order'.

As biomedicine established itself in the nineteenth century, health became defined increasingly against a standard of normality and in terms of the absence of disease or infirmity. Pathogenesis – the search for the origins of disease – became the cornerstone of medicine. In contrast to older forms of humoral medicine in which the balance, vigour and health of the person were paramount, biomedical practice focused on the impersonal search for the 'lesion' (Armstrong 1987).

The power of biomedicine rests in its monopolistic right to 'produce' the body by naming its parts (anatomy), its functions (physiology) and – most importantly – its lesions (pathology). This focus on abnormality and its elimination meant that the 'person' – or what Jewson (1976) called the 'sick man' – disappeared from biomedical language and practice. The sick person became reduced to and understood in terms of the disease that she or he suffered from, and biomedicine engaged not with people, but with damaged tissues and diagnostic labels.

As the 'sick man' disappeared, so too did 'bedside medicine' (Jewson 1976). The intimacy of the patients' 'natural' environment was replaced by the hospital, which became the primary site of medical practice. Before the rise of the hospital as *the* therapeutic space, a great deal of attention was paid to patients' distinctive accounts of their conditions. A vast range of biographical detail was considered important to a full and proper understanding of patients' medical condition, and the home (or bedside) was regarded as the appropriate place for medical work.

Modern 'hospital medicine' put an end to personalized, patient-centred practice and secured a change from a conception of disease as a disturbance in the balance of life to one that focused on it as a localized pathology. Patients became 'cases' who were not unique. They were defined (by diagnosis) as belonging to a specific category of disease derived from the general body of abstract clinical knowledge. Patients' stories about their lives became much less important than the objective signs of disease that the physicians would read from their patients' disturbed bodies. Of what relevance are patients' narratives when disease 'is regarded as the consequence of certain malfunctions of the human body conceptualized as a biochemical machine' (Turner 1995: 9)?

By the 1870s biomedicine had developed a sophisticated scientific conception of causality which became known as the 'doctrine of specific aetiology' (Scambler 1991: 19). This doctrine locates disease in the pathology of human tissues. It assumes 'that all human dysfunctions might eventually be traced to . . . specific causal mechanisms within the organism' (Turner 1995: 9). This is a uni-causal model in which a specific disease is associated with a single cause and a specific germ or microbe is regarded as the causal agent. Such a notion of causality helps to sustain a conception of the body as a pre-social, natural, passive entity.

Biopsychosocial medicine proposes a holistic practice and a multi-causal model. It developed out of the limitations of biomedicine, some of which have just been identified. The Achilles' heel of biomedicine is that it reduces human life to biological life and so privileges biological 'explanations at the expense of social, cultural and biographical' ones (Atkinson 1988: 180). As René Dubos (1960: 77) put it, biomedicine has the 'tendency to study man as a non-thinking, non-feeling animal'. It is a victim of its Cartesian origins. In other words, the central limitation of biomedicine is biological reductionism. For biopsychosocial medicine people are more than bodies. Human existence is, simultaneously, biological, psychological and social. A healthy life suggests not only a healthy body, but also a healthy mind and a safe environment. Health therefore becomes a concept that embraces all the dimensions of human existence (Hughes 1996). This argument suggests that health and illness – indeed, existence itself – can be explained (and experienced, perhaps simultaneously) on three levels – the somatic, the psychic and the social. Healthcare practice must, therefore, be dedicated to intervention at whatever levels are appropriate to the enhancement of the well-being of the patient. Biopsychosocial medicine is described as holistic because it does not reduce health to its biological dimensions. It is concerned with 'total health' (Nettleton 1995).

As biomedicine begins to conceive of health in holistic terms rather than as the absence of corporeal infirmity, it must, of necessity, expand its knowledge base beyond the traditional biomedical sciences. Healthcare professionals now meet the disciplines of psychology and sociology in their education and training, and these subjects, in theory, provide the platform for overcoming biological reductionism. As medicine expands what it means by a healthy life, it demands a much expanded epistemology. Not only the body, but also its behaviours and the spaces in which it moves, become medicalized. The biopsychosocial model envisages multiple, even unlimited, sites for intervention and surveillance. The expanded concept of health knowledge, which supersedes its reductionist and mechanical counterpart, implies a body that is active in the production of its own well-being.

It has become increasingly difficult to sustain the notion that the body is a machine and that its health is solely dependent on its repair. The mechanical metaphor ignores the thinking, feeling and social aspects of healthy human existence (Mishler *et al.* 1981), and biomedicine feels compelled to embrace these social and emotional dimensions of health. In so doing, the passive body of biomedicine is slowly replaced by the active body of biopsychosocial medicine.

The vigilant body of biopsychosocial medicine

The shift from biomedicine to biopsychosocial medicine is partly a consequence of the incredulity and scepticism that surround science and professional expertise in contemporary times. By focusing on health maintenance as opposed to the identification and elimination of disease, the role of healthcare expertise can be recast as advisory. As people are expected to take responsibility for their own health and to practise healthy behaviour, everyday life becomes regarded as an arena of risk and preventive action (Giddens 1991; Williams and Calnan 1996). This shift has prompted scholars such as Meg Stacey (1994: 89) to comment that lay people 'are as much producers as consumers of health care'. Indeed, they can be regarded as 'medical auxiliaries' involved 'in the division of medical work' (Pinell 1996). The vigilant lay body, which practises self-care through self-surveillance (Foucault 1990), is at the heart of contemporary healthcare practice.

Buried in the notion of the vigilant lay body is a concession to a multi-dimensional view of the causes of health and disease. Germs make us ill, but so too do stress, unhealthy activities, poverty, unemployment and so on. Not only do we need to guard against invasive microbes, we must also organize our lives to maximize our immunity against a risk-laden social world. The doctrine of specific aetiology is far too unilateral to account for contemporary patterns of morbidity and mortality. In what has been called the 'epidemiological clinic' of late modernity (Bunton and Burrows 1995), the socio-moral question about how we maintain our bodies has become more important than the technical question about eliminating disease after it has become established in the human body. The range of causal possibilities for both health and illness has consequently proliferated. As the social world becomes constituted as a massive space for preventive action in which risk is all around us, then the uni-causal doctrine that underpinned biomedicine seems less convincing.

This transformation in medical practice is also linked to significant changes in the pattern of disease. Biomedicine was at its height during the last part of the nineteenth century and the early part of the twentieth century, when infectious diseases were the major killers in western societies (McKeown 1976). Today, in countries such as Britain, death from infectious disease is relatively rare. The major killers are cancer, heart disease, stroke and accidents. There has been, therefore, a massive change in the epidemiological map. Indeed, Anselm Strauss *et al.* (1985) have argued that we have entered a 'new biological era'. As the pattern of disease has shifted from the acute and the infectious to the chronic and limiting, the pathogenic and curative emphasis of biomedicine has become increasingly untenable. The pattern of contemporary disease encourages the search for salutogens – the things, behaviours and spaces that contribute to well-being. The discourse of health maintenance raises questions about how we behave, the kinds of things that we consume, the risks we are prepared to take or avoid and the 'therapeutic' status of the social spaces in which bodies work, rest and play. The problem of heart disease, for example, has been recast as a lifestyle problem. Biomedical solutions are a last resort when strategies of health maintenance fail.

As health maintenance – as opposed to curative – strategies emerge as the priority in contemporary patterns of health care, then responsibility for health shifts from the professional to the lay person and the relationship between these two parties in the medical encounter becomes less entrenched and polarized. Biomedicine deskilled ordinary people by expecting them to be passive in relation to their health and deferential in their relationships with health professionals. The idea of 'doctor knows best' was a recipe for professional paternalism. The patient was expected to play the infant role and the professional to act out the adult one. One was expected to put one's body in the hands of expertise (Parsons 1951). Biomedicine absolved the lay person from responsibility for illness. The contemporary climate, which valorizes the vigilant lay body, is less forgiving.

At the beginning of the twenty-first century, authority – be it medical, parental or political – can no longer command unequivocal respect or compliance. The 1960s put an end to that. Authority was there to serve and be questioned, not to follow blindly. Lay people and patients began to ask questions, to expect service and to recognize the validity of their own perspectives. There can be no doubt that this apparent democratization of the relationship between professional and patient suited western governments intent on reducing public expenditure and squeezing the welfare state. The ideas of self-care and health maintenance as the responsibility of the lay person rather than the professional became, in the 1980s, important ideological tools in the privatization of healthcare activities. Illich (1977: 6) identifies this shift as a sociological landmark: 'The age of disabling professions ... when people had "problems", experts had "solutions" and scientists measured imponderables such as "abilities" and "needs". This age is now at an end.' In the post-professional age the state – no longer the 'nanny' of old – expects its 'active citizens' to take responsibility for their own bodies. The lay person has been transformed into the rational consumer and medicine has been subjected to political, social, cultural and economic forces that have driven it further into the logic of commercialism. In Britain, the *Patient's Charter* (Department of Health

1991) is the manifesto of this transformation from the passive to the consuming body. As consumers, patients can no longer be objectified as compliant bodies. Lay power proletarianizes professionalism and transforms its actions into goods and services. Consumerism undermines medical dominance and demands partnership rather than paternalism from professionals (Klein 1989). Health professionals can no longer expect to work with and on docile bodies. The patient has become a person and this new status opens up the psychosocial dimensions of health, illness and the body to new forms of social control and medical surveillance (Peterson and Bunton 1997).

Biomedicine has long been regarded by sociologists as an institution of social control (Zola 1972). Feminist scholars have been particularly productive in charting the story of medical control over women's lives and bodies (for example, see Martin 1989). Despite its claim to scientific neutrality, modern medicine has been involved in the disciplining and surveillance of populations (Foucault 1976b). It is an important player in the production of social order. Medicine is deeply involved in the regulation of people and the government of bodies (Turner 1992, 1996). By drawing lifestyle and environment into the domain of health, biopsychosocial medicine extends and deepens these possibilities. In the contemporary, secular, deregulated world, a good deal of the policing of human behaviour – which is traditionally invested in the powers of religion and law – is carried out in the name of health. The contemporary physician is as likely to 'dispense' 'healthy' information or 'prescribe' behavioural change as he or she is to treat one's condition or offer the instant solution of 'magic bullets'. Biopsychosocial medicine, therefore, involves the medicalization of lifestyle, consumption and social space and it does so through its various manifestos for healthy living (Bunton *et al.* 1995). Eating, drinking, sleeping, leisure activities, sexual behaviour, cities and communities have all come under the jurisdiction of medical regulation. The good life has become the healthy life and each and every one of us is expected to integrate the codes, conducts and prescriptions of such a life into our daily activities. As medicine extends its gaze beyond the body, its power disperses throughout the social body. Medical knowledge, often in the form of behavioural prescriptions, challenges the population to be healthy, to adopt healthy behaviours and to choose healthy places to live and work. Biopsychosocial medicine, with its exhortations to choose health and actively practise self-care, is well suited to the information society (Lyon 1994), in which technologies of communication provide populations with advice about how to live and how to avoid risk.

Yet, just as everyday behaviour, or embodied activity, has become a target for healthcare intervention, so too have the spaces in which bodies move. There has been a significant expansion in the geography of healthcare activity. Nettleton (1995: 248) notes some of the ways in which biopsychosocial medicine transcends the geographical limitations of biomedicine:

First, it involved a new way of organizing health care that related to community. Functioning beyond the walls of the hospital, it acted as a coordinating centre for those who sought out and monitored disease. Second, the medical gaze was diverted from the interior of the physical body to the spaces between bodies. Pathology was not localized and static but found to travel throughout the social body and so there was a need to focus on contacts, relationships and home visits. . . . Third, as surveillance extended throughout the community the emphasis began to shift from those who were ill to those who were potentially ill.

The community has become a therapeutic site in which relationships and space are targets for healthcare intervention. The logic extends to the environment, particularly urban space, which is manifest in the concept of the 'healthy city' (Ashton and Seymour 1988). This massive relocation of healthcare activity has been neatly summed up as a 'shift from bodies in hospitals to people in communities' (Nettleton and Burrows 1994: 3). The phrase suggests the (potential) omnipresence of therapeutic sites and possibilities. It also suggests a much extended conception of the subject of healthcare expertise and a reworking of the definition of health as the relationship between the body and the social world. The biopsychosocial body is locked into a 'systems theory' of health in which the body, the mind and social location are interacting subsystems in the complex web that makes up the multiple determinants of health.

Public health, health promotion and the disciplined body

If biomedicine was concerned, primarily, with the medicalization of the body, then biopsychosocial medicine – in the name of the health of the body – extends the process of medicalization into lifestyle and social organization. The 'new public health', and health promotion in particular, is the key mediator in this process of bodily regulation (Lupton 1995). In practice, health promotion tends to focus on transformations of lifestyle rather than changes in social structure. Health promotion preaches the precepts of a proper, medically informed relationship to one's body.

In a partial sense, health promotion embodies a promise of release from medicine. Regimes of health maintenance imply the possibility of independence from medical expertise through the hard work of self-mastery and bodily regulation. If one is, for example, willing to transform the rhythms of leisure and the patterns of consumption, then freedom from heart disease and circulatory problems is – more or less – promoted as the outcome. The encouragement to exercise, for example, envisages a profound transformation of leisure – from relaxation to working out, from rest to activity. Glassner (1989: 187) writes:

At the postmodern health club – filled with glimmering machines which disaffirm their modernism by being labour-making devices – leisure is work, impulses are harnessed into repetitions per minute, and the conscience, now of the body as much as it is of the soul, is only as strong as its owner's heart and as firm as her thighs.

It costs a lot to join the postmodern health club but one is paying for more than firm thighs. One is paying for a 'good' body. In contemporary consumer culture, to look good is to feel good is to be good. The outer body, when healthy and beautiful, confirms the positive moral disposition of the inner self (Featherstone 1991a). One is paying – if one can afford to do so – for access to facilities that are essential to success. Contemporary projects of self-identity are based on the moralization, aestheticization and medicalization of self through body work. Health promotion discourse is tuned into this project and it enables medicine to engage productively with aesthetic and ethical trends in contemporary culture. The ethical self (of both health promotion and contemporary culture) appears in a particular shape – in fact, 'in shape'. The embodiment of the ethical self is toned, ordered and visible as a 'good' body, and the good body is indicative of the subjection of self to regimes of discipline. The firmness of one's body is a testimony to oneself as an ethical subject. The firm body sends a clear message: its 'owner' is one who applies the codes and commandments of contemporary medical wisdom to him or herself. To practise healthy behaviour is to improve one's 'physical capital' (Bourdieu 1984) and, therefore, enhance one's social and moral worth.

The path to ethical self-regulation is one that is signposted by health promotion discourse which translates and simplifies medical wisdom into dicta of conduct. These provide a code and a set of behaviours that are useful for the management of one's daily existence. They promote a 'regimen' of mundane healthy activities. It is striking that the scope and nature of this regimen is not that different from the one that Foucault (1986: 101) describes as a model of ancient prescriptions for conduct. He refers to Book VI of Hippocrates' *Epidemics*, in which a conceptual map of regimen exhorts people to take care in relation to exercise, food, drink, sleep and sexual behaviour. Regimen refers to the management of everyday conduct or daily habits. Today we would probably invoke the concept of lifestyle. Foucault argues that the health maintenance strategies of the ancients are 'an art of living' – indeed, 'a whole manner of forming oneself as a subject who had a proper, necessary and sufficient concern for one's body' (1986: 108).

Health promotion offers prescriptions for behaviour. It comprises a set of prescriptive texts that constitute a practical philosophy for the 'civilized' government of the body and the construction of ethical subjectivity. It is concerned, primarily, with the conduct of life, with 'well-being' and with 'self-mastery'. Health promotion as a set of educational statements and images is a discourse of moral regulation (Lupton

1995), with an investment in the production of self-regulated bodies and populations. Thus, the prescriptions for behaviour embedded in health promotion texts are both medical and moral. Once again we can draw a parallel with Foucault's work on conduct in the classical age. In *The History of Sexuality* he examines a number of classical texts which he describes as 'prescriptive texts' or 'prescriptive discourses' (1986: 249). These are:

> texts which no matter what their form – dialogues, treatises, collections of precepts, letters – sought primarily to propose rules of . . . behaviour. Such texts acted as *operators* enabling individuals to question their own conduct in order to build their own personalities – the very stuff of character making.
>
> (Merquior 1985: 126; our italics)

Contemporary health promotion texts embody this prescriptive role with respect to conduct and its link to 'character'. The rules and codes are established in moral-semantic form as behaviours and actions (and even places) that are good for you or bad for you. Given that these prescriptions are derived from the scientific discoveries of medicine, health promotion might be described as its moral dispensary. It does not, however, dispense tablets or medications but rather words to live by. It is medicine reduced to aphorisms of conduct that encourage people to develop a *proper* relationship to their bodies. Health promotion is based on the assumption of the informed lay person who is active in the production of the healthy self.

The promotion of knowledge about health is not intended to be didactic, but it does tend to be presented as interpretive repertoires for living which are based on rules of conduct. The health promotion messages are 'dos and don'ts' – if not commandments, then moral imperatives that trade on aesthetic outcomes. They often have a sound-bite form and can easily be reduced to watchwords and beatitudes. They are also practical guides. For example, health promotion discourses about smoking tell us not only to give it up but how to do it. The disciplines and skills of abnegation are presented in the form of manuals (like car manuals) from which one can learn how to put into practice the doctrine of self-care. One is expected to quit the weed because its use is linked to disease, death, antisocial behaviour and moral failure and one is given instructions on the techniques for overcoming the irrational cravings of the body. The wayward body has to be brought to heel because the price for failing to do so is so high. One is encouraged to critically interrogate one's actual behaviour against the codes of an ethical ideal.

The efforts of health promotion are, therefore, invariably narratives of transformation through self-regulation. One is encouraged to make a transformation with oneself as the object of change and, more often than not, some ascetic practice dominates the mode of transformation. The not-so-perfect body is expected to make a journey of self-transformation that terminates in the ethical self, in self-mastery. This is symbolized in practice by the sublime moment of success when the addiction is brought under control, the target weight achieved, the finishing line of the marathon crossed. The reward for success is the personal and public recognition of one's moral status or moral rehabilitation. The badge of self-mastery is the purified, transformed, disciplined, orderly, ethical body. The health norms of contemporary society are manifest in health promotion. As such, they form a new regime of self-surveillance based on the medicalization of lifestyle and behaviour. They construct the ethical, self-regulated subject as the embodiment of self-mastery and offer the deviant body strategies and repertoires for aesthetic and moral transformation. These processes imply a change in the meaning of disease.

Disease – in at least some of its manifestations – can now be regarded as a failure of health maintenance, a sign of an improper relationship to one's body and to what one does with it. The self is problematized by the appearance of disease because it is a sign of weakness, of lack of control, of self-neglect, of a person in moral debt. The right to appeal to the public purse, to the acute health services, for resources to tackle the invaded body, is becoming more dependent on normative – as opposed to clinical – assessment. One has failed to put into practice the moral prescriptions of health promotion, so why should the community take responsibility for that failure. The trauma of disease can therefore be interpreted as a payback for a bad diet, for too many hours spent slumped on the couch glued to the TV, for the long years consuming coffin nails, for those lost weekends in the arms of demon drink, for that quick fuck without a condom. Each activity carried a highly publicized risk, a health warning. Those who have ignored the dangers get what they deserve.

In the image and information economies of late capitalism, the rules of self-care and health maintenance are made as transparent as possible. They are dispensed, in people-friendly form, by the apparatuses of health promotion. In theory, therefore, lifestyle can be managed to avoid risk. Healthy activities and objects can be selected in preference to their pathogenic, dangerous counterparts. One can be safe in one's own hands, providing one follows the rules of conduct and mobilizes the appropriate moral prescriptions. Like good and evil, in pre-secular, pre-modern societies, the therapeutic and the anti-therapeutic are omnipresent, manifest and easily identifiable in actions and in objects of material culture. Health promotion structures its messages on the distinction between good and bad and assumes a rational, unitary subject who can be ethical by acts of informed will (Lupton 1995). These assumptions are normative and utopian. They mobilize the medical in pursuit of the ethical and aesthetic, in a way that positions power productively and fairly unambiguously on the terrain of everyday actions and behaviours. Even if one resists the rules and moral prescriptions of health promotion, one cannot help but engage with them. Indeed, they engage with us as the normative, narrative codes that underpin proper bodily practices. As such, they are thoroughly implicated in the construction of self-identity (Giddens 1991) and the body projects that are testimony to the 'unfinished' nature of embodiment in the contemporary world (Shilling 1993).

Breasts and testicles: the medicalization of lay tactility and the dispersal of medical power

The touch of the health professional is supposed to be informed by 'affective neutrality' or emotional distance. In the vast majority of cases it probably is. The health professional has access to the most intimate parts of the body. This privilege is predicated on the application of a special type of touch, one in which emotional distance defuses the ambiguities and tensions of physical proximity. During the process of professional socialization the health professional learns to objectify the patient. This probably helps the professional to internalize the unwritten rules of physical engagement, so that in the actual medical encounter the definition of touch brooks no dubiety. However, one can argue that this specialist form of tactility is beginning to be dispersed throughout the lay population and is most manifest in the growth of self-examination as a legitimate form of lay health work.

The jury is out with regard to the clinical effectiveness of self-examination of breasts and testicles (Austoker and Evans 1992). However, the consensus is that it cannot do any harm and may well, in some cases, reduce the time between onset and diagnosis of cancer in these sites. Information about self-examination is readily available in clinics and hospitals in the standard 'how to' format. What this information does not say, however, is that the practice of self-examination turns the lay person into an auxiliary diagnostician. There is implied in this process a reorganization of embodiment, or at least a reorganization of how we are expected to know and touch our bodies. Although we can and do experience our bodies as objects (Leder 1990), particularly when ill or damaged, the frame of reference through which our bodies are known to us, or *lived*, is usually personal and subjective. The idea of self-examination implies, however, that we must apply a clinical and professional frame of reference to ourselves and thus experience our carnality as a sort of fleshy otherness. In touching our own breasts or testicles we are expected to forgo the onanistic and pleasurable element associated with these erogenous zones and adopt a medical form of tactility in which we exteriorize ourselves. In these acts of vigilance, in which our health is, quite literally, in our own hands, we are expected to turn the medical gaze on ourselves. This is a classic example of self-surveillance (Foucault 1980) – the moment in which social control becomes self-control: 'Just a gaze. An inspecting

gaze, a gaze which each individual under its weight will end by exteri-
orizing to the point that he is his own overseer, each individual thus
exercising this surveillance over and against himself' (Foucault 1980:
155).

In the contemporary world the logic of medicalization extends into
the private world of self-reflection, encouraging new forms of body
work in which medical skills are applied by lay persons to themselves.
Through its ever-growing imperative to inform, medical discourse
empowers us to inspect ourselves and provides us with the tools –
once jealously held only by the state registered – of bodily vigilance
and self-examination.

> Bodily manifestations usually considered innocuous by lay people
> have to be dramatized in order to give them another meaning ie:
> possible signals of an early cancer. This dramatization takes place
> within the dynamics of medicalization. Its aim is to turn every-
> one into a sentry, a potential patient looking after his own body
> and ready to consult his practitioner as soon as he picks up on
> a suspicious signal. The explicit objective is, through adequate
> education, to medicalize the way that each person looks at his
> own body.
>
> (Pinell 1996: 13)

The informed patient or potential patient knows how to read his or
her body as a medical text, to screen him or herself by self-examination
and to conclude – should bodily norms seem distorted – with a pre-
liminary and provisional diagnosis. Self-examination or learning to
relate to one's body as a medical text – that is, as an object of para-
professional self-scrutiny – is a significant aspect of the medicalization of everyday life that arises as medicine disperses its knowledge
throughout the social body.

The notion of a vigilant, active, lay body that mobilizes medical
information and advice – be it around issues of health maintenance or
self-examination – in the name of health work has significant implications for the nature of medical power. The re-ordering and transformation of medical power has a strong affinity with Jean Baudrillard's
(1988a: 107) description of the new form of American power:

> ... America is no longer the monopolistic centre of world power.
> This is not because it has lost its power, but simply because there
> is no centre anymore. It has ... become the orbit of an imaginary
> power to which everyone now refers. From the point of view of
> competition, hegemony and imperialism, it has lost its ground,
> but from the exponential point of view it has gained some: take
> the unintelligible rise of the dollar for example which bears no
> relation to any economic supremacy ... or even – and why not –
> the world wide success of *Dallas*. America has retained power,
> both political and cultural, but it is now power as a special effect.

The idea of power diversified and without a centre seems to fit contemporary medicine and is consistent with the idea that medical work has become displaced and diversified, a matter as much for lay vigilance as the application of expertise. In the form of TV programmes and Coca-Cola, America is everywhere, colonizing every reach of the globe with the typical symbols of its consumer culture. Likewise, medicine is omnipresent in the form of information that we use to guide us through the risks, pitfalls and problems of life. It is the source of the good life, the means to longevity, health and fitness (Glassner 1992), be it 'natural' or cosmetic (K. Davis 1995). It is our companion in decisions that need to be taken about eating, sleeping, drinking and sexual relations, and it informs how we run and plan our cities and communities (Bunton *et al.* 1995). As health work has become 'decentred', then 'power relations are rendered invisible, and are dispersed, being voluntarily perpetuated by subjects upon themselves' (Lupton 1994: 32).

Conclusion

In the 'regime of total health' (Armstrong 1987) the subject of healthcare activity is massively expanded. Even though the body is the focus of all this activity the psychosocial dimensions of health and illness are considered to be integral to the regime. The embrace of biomedicine and public health gives birth to biopsychosocial medicine. This is a model of medicine in which health is conceived in terms of the interaction between biological, psychological and social systems. It becomes difficult to distinguish between the clinical and the social because the world is divided into actions, things and spaces that are either 'good for you' or 'bad for you'. As the social forces that act on the body and embodied behaviour itself are recognized as belonging to the 'regime of total health', new forms of therapeutic space and action can be continuously invented. Nothing, in theory, falls outside the orbit of healthcare work because the healthy subject is ecologically situated. If the problems and patterns of living are implicated in the causation of disease and the maintenance of health, then the clinic is compelled to escape the confines of its specialist space and subject (the body) and spread its gaze over the complex canvas of everyday life. Every behaviour, thing and space is scrutinized for its salutary potential, and for the support that it can offer to the body in its battle to survive. Furthermore, the agency of the body is valorized because health is transformed into an individual responsibility. The old passive body of biomedicine is dead and buried.

Understood as a biological object, the medical body has remained, in some ways, stable and predictable. For example, Laqueur (1990) has argued that since the latter part of the eighteenth century, medical science has maintained the view that the sexes are opposite. It is only recently that challenges to this hegemonic perspective have been mounted. Feminists such as Elizabeth Grosz (1994) have suggested that the classification of bodies by 'opposed sex' misrepresents the character of embodied difference. Sex is unstable, indeterminate, relational, caught up in and produced out of relations of power. Even biology itself is generating new ways of thinking about the body and, indeed, life itself. Molecular biology, biotechnology and the Human Genome Project are beginning to spell out a 'radical revision of the very notion of corporeality' (Rose 1998: 161). One wonders what medical practice will look like after the new biology has given it a thorough theoretical make-over. If social constructionist arguments also have an influence on it, it may be difficult to recognize.

Further reading

For an interesting discussion of the biomedical body Leder's edited collection *The Body in Medical Thought and Practice* (1992) is useful. The sociology of the body – and its debates and theoretical richness – has, of late, become more integrated into the sociology of health and illness. *Regulating Bodies: Essays in Medical Sociology* (1992) by Bryan Turner is an early and valuable example of this symbiosis. Deborah Lupton in *Medicine as Culture: Illness, Disease and the Body in Western Societies* (1994) uses a constructionist account to both analyse and critique the medical body, whereas Sarah Nettleton in *The Sociology of Health and Illness* (1995) and Bryan Turner in the second edition of *Medical Power and Social Knowledge* (1995) have both produced textbooks in which the sociology of the body plays a significant role in delineating the scope of sociological debate about medicine, health and illness. Wendy Seymour's essay on rehabilitation, *Remaking the Body* (1998), is well grounded in a phenomenological sociology of the body. In her recent work on immunology – *Flexible Bodies* (1994) – the feminist scholar Emily Martin provides a fascinating analysis of the links between broad social transformations and lay accounts of the importance of 'agile' immune systems. There is, of course, a well established literature in which medical control over women's bodies is a central theme. It seems almost offensive to single out and recommend a text from this rich tradition, but one cannot go wrong, as a point of departure, with Emily Martin's *The Woman in the Body* (1989). With respect to the male body, Sabo and Gordon's edited volume, *Men's Health and Illness: Gender, Power and the Body* (1995), provides an interesting introduction to embodied masculinities. The 'new public health' and health promotion signal the arrival of the healthy body as a product of the active and vigilant lay subject. Of the literature in this field two books stand out: Deborah Lupton's Foucauldian volume *The Imperative of Health: Public Health and the Regulated Body* (1995) and the collection edited by Bunton, Nettleton and Burrows entitled

The Sociology of Health Promotion (1995). For those who wish to learn more about the application of constructionist theory to the medical body, then *Foucault, Health and Medicine* (1997) edited by Peterson and Bunton and Nick Fox's rather more esoteric work *Postmodernism, Sociology and Health* (1993) will both repay scholarly attention.

Disabled bodies

KEVIN PATERSON AND BILL HUGHES

Introduction

This chapter considers bodies that have often had a liminal or token presence in sociological discourse. We will call them 'disabled bodies'. It should be noted at the outset, however, that the two words that form the couplet are uneasy bedfellows because disability, as we will see, has more to do with social exclusion and oppression than with corporeal status. By and large, sociology has accepted the hegemonic notion of the 'disabled body' as 'deficit' and 'invalidity'. Disability is perceived as pre-social and hence as best understood by the disciplines of medicine and psychology (Oliver 1990; Barton 1996; Barnes *et al.* 1999). Sociology has failed to redeem itself even where it might be expected to do so. Disability studies treats both the sociology of medicine and the sociology of the body with some suspicion. Medical sociologists have insisted on conflating analysis of the disabled body and the sick body (Barnes and Mercer 1996; Shakespeare and Watson 1997). For their part, sociologists of the body have been keen to rethink female, black and gay bodies, but have largely ignored the corporeality of disabled people (L. Davis 1995; Abberley 1997; Paterson and Hughes 1999). It has been left to disabled activists and their allies to provide a critical, radical and structural analysis of disability (see Barton and Oliver 1997).

For (bio)medicine, disability is reduced to physicality but in disability studies the body has been displaced as the central focus of analysis. However, as we will see in the first and final sections of this chapter, in disability studies the body is now returning from exile and it is doing so as an object of sociological rather than medical analysis. With the exception of Wendy Seymour's work (1998), the attempt to develop an embodied view of disability is emerging from within the framework of disability studies. This development envisages what has been called a social model or sociology of impairment (Shakespeare and Watson 1995a; Hughes and Paterson 1997). Despite the general neglect of disability by the sociology of the body, the sociology of impairment is indebted to its conceptual armoury and springs from attention to the work of Turner (1992, 1996) and Shilling (1993), among others. Following Turner's (1992, 1996) reference to 'somatic society', and in light of the recognition of the social and cultural import of the 'somatic turn', there has been an attempt in disability studies to critique the modernist separation of the body from politics (Corker 1999; Hughes 1999). If in late capitalism the body or embodied subject has become a significant site for social, political and cultural activity, then it is important for disability studies to revisit one of its central axioms – that is, the distinction between disability and impairment. The final section of this chapter will attend to this issue.

For disabled people, the 'project' of modernity has not been particularly auspicious. This chapter is about bodies that have been 'stripped of agency' and about how those same bodies are struggling to recover it. In the story that unfolds capitalism and medicine are central protagonists in the long assault on the dignity of disabled people, and disabled people are the central characters in the struggle to restore it. This struggle has been about emancipation from oppression, establishing claims to citizenship and full social participation, and transforming disability from a 'spoilt' (Goffman 1971a) to a positive identity. Its effect has been to begin to reconstitute the experience of disability. As a consequence, the struggle seems to be entering a new phase. The movement of disabled people is rethinking its epistemological reliance on the economic determinism of the social model of disability. Engagement with issues of culture, language, difference and the relationship between embodiment and emancipation are signs of new momentum in the movement.

From dependency to pride

The past two decades have been witness to a politicization of disability and there has been a seismic shift in its conceptualization. It has been transformed from an individual or medical problem into a civil rights issue. Disabled people have organized themselves intellectually and politically. Disability studies has become the intellectual core of the disability movement and the social model of disability has become its theoretical voice. This model was developed to challenge the individual or medical model of disability in which disability is conceived largely in terms of somatic and intellectual abnormality (Oliver 1983).

Disabled people are entering the new millennium as a group collect-
ively constituted in a new social movement (Davis 1993; Campbell
and Oliver 1996; Oliver 1996a). Disabled people, like women, black
and gay people, are involved in a struggle for human rights. They
demand emancipation from social oppression and exclusion. In the
context of exclusionary social structures (rooted in industrialization
and the medicalization of disability in the nineteenth century), the
response to people with impairments has been to regard them as
unable to live up to – and to cope with – the demands of a 'normal
life'. They have been constructed as the 'other', as 'flawed' (Hevey 1992).
They have been dispatched – so the story goes – to 'special' segregated
establishments for their own physical, psychological and social well-
being. Disabled activists have defined this response as (dis)ablism, a
form of institutional discrimination equivalent to sexism, heterosexism
and racism (Barnes 1994). The disabled people's movement has its
(s)heroes in the same way that other movements have theirs. However, they are not saluted because they have overcome the tragedy of
a medical problem, but because they have challenged oppression and
struggled against the charitable gaze of bourgeois paternalism.

Disabled people are (and have been throughout modernity) depicted
as dependent individuals waiting patiently or petulantly for care, cure
or charity. The elimination of this infantilizing portrayal of disability
is a central tenet of the disabled people's movement. Rather than
accept the injunction to 'pass as normal', the movement has adopted
the Gay Rights concept of 'pride' in difference and the practice of
'coming out'. The image of disabled bodies chained to buses, voicing
sentiments such as 'piss on pity' and 'rights not charity', is a powerful
one. The struggle for equal rights is a direct attack on the disablist
notion that disabled people are nothing more than victims of defective
bodies.

Involvement in street protest reverses the idea that disabled people
are content to wait for charity to be bestowed on them. Disability
pride is a concept that treats the ethos of 'normality' and the practices
of normalization with contempt. These notions are indicative of an
aestheticized value system that questions the worth of people with
impairments. 'Coming out' transforms the ideology of the disabled
body as deficit into a statement of collective muscularity. Indeed, the
concepts of political 'movement' and 'activist' challenge the notion of
the 'dependent invalid'. They symbolize agency and autonomy.

The dynamic for this challenge to discourses of passivity, charity
and medicalization dates back to the 1970s and the formation of the
Union of Physically Impaired Against Segregation (UPIAS). The UPIAS
– a UK disabled people's collective – advocated collective, organized
struggle. Disabled people were encouraged to fight for full social participation (Pagel 1988). Although they broadly accepted the medical
definition of impairment as the lack of a limb or a function of a
'crippled' body, the early activists of the UPIAS reversed the meaning
of disability (Barnes *et al.* 1999). Their 'manifesto', *The Fundamental*

Principles of Disability, redefined disability as 'the disadvantage or restriction of activity caused by a contemporary organization which takes no or little account of people who have physical impairments and thus excludes them from participation in the mainstream of social activities' (UPIAS 1976: 14).

The UPIAS broke with the 'tradition' that had constituted disability as 'dependency' and 'deficit' and provided a definition of disability that reflected the standpoint of disabled people. A new voice – one that had been silenced and was expected to remain so – cleared its throat and in so doing reconfigured the map of meaning in which exile and restriction had been reference points for disabled lives. Medical definitions of disability had been invalidating. But disability defined as a restrictive situation imposed on people with impairments by the patterns and expectations of an (dis)ablist society embodied the promise of emancipation. Disability became defined as a particular form of social oppression.

During the past 20 years the strategy identified and exemplified by the UPIAS – progress through organized, collective action – has developed rapidly (Hasler 1993; Campbell and Oliver 1996). Disabled people have never been so politically visible as they were in the 1990s. Direct action and political demonstrations have forced politicians, the media and the public to confront the realities of inaccessible public transport, welfare cuts and institutional discrimination. Furthermore, the liberating outlook of pride and self-respect has helped disabled people to challenge eugenicist concepts of 'quality of life' at a time when genetic testing, selective abortion and euthanasia threatens the very existence of people with impaired bodies.

Disabled people's struggle for emancipation is embodied. The assertion that the disabled body is a badge of pride rather than a mark of disgrace signals the fact that the body is not apolitical. The disabled body has been moulded (and distorted) by dominant norms and practices but it is now being transformed by a manifesto of self-respect that brings disabled people out into spaces from which they have been hitherto excluded (Paterson and Hughes 1999). The modernist response to disabled people's bodies has been to segregate and conceal them, to make them symbols of shame and objects of fear. This disablism has usually been dressed in the language and practice of care, rehabilitation and charity. The contemporary politics of disability challenges the infantilization and medicalization of disability. It seeks to reclaim bodies that have been oppressed and excluded.

Since the discrimination and exclusion faced by disabled people has been justified, historically, by biological arguments, it made good political sense for the disabled people's movement to ignore the body and its impairments and to focus on a structural analysis of the social causes of disablement. This priority is rooted theoretically in the work of Hunt (1966), the UPIAS (1976), Vic Finkelstein (1980) and Michael Oliver (1983, 1990). These authors have claimed that disability is socially produced, and have fashioned a materialist theory that separates out bodily impairment from socially produced disablement. This dualistic view of the social and the biological as binary opposites is one of the maxims on which disability studies is founded. It has facilitated a de-biologization of discourses around disablement. As Shakespeare (1992: 40) states, 'The achievement of the disability movement has been to break the link between our bodies and our social situation, and to focus on the real cause of disability, i.e. discrimination and prejudice.' In the next section we will turn to an exploration of the origins of this link that has been broken.

Disability, medicine and medical sociology

The idea of biophysical 'normality' is a core value in western culture (L. Davis 1995). Individuals are bombarded with images of the perfect body (Stone 1995; Wendell 1996). Success is correlated with a bodily aesthetic that is narrowly prescriptive in terms of weight, shape, posture and gait. Capitalism demands individual economic productivity and this enshrines the notion of biophysical fitness, and its fulfilment as a key element in the quest for fashionable self-identity. Scientific medicine provides the means for measuring 'fitness' and identifying deviations from its statistical norm. Consequently, the hegemonic notion of the disabled body constructs it in terms of corporeal or intellectual 'deficit'. To overcome this deficit, the disabled body requires the services of scientific medicine and rehabilitation.

Rehabilitative and therapeutic approaches to disability and impairment concentrate on rectifying a perceived mental or physical 'flaw' that prevents or hampers an individual's ability to function 'normally'. These professional practices focus on cerebral and anatomical functioning and how they are disrupted by certain 'disabling conditions'. Ability is defined as a 'performance' that matches the norms of gait, posture, stature and speech, and disability acquires meaning as the 'botching' of these norms. The traditional goal of therapy is to determine ways in which the performance of a disabled person can be restored to something approximating 'normality'. This approach centres on the concept of individual adjustment. The disabled person must come to terms, both physically and psychologically, with his or her disabled body. This and the task of restoring normal function and appearance are the purposes of rehabilitation.

Over the past 50 years, there has been a good deal of theorizing in the social sciences about disability and impairment (Barnes 1998). Although this has spawned a critique of rehabilitation practice, most of this academic work has not sought to overhaul medicalized and individualized conceptions of disability. The alternative insights into and definitions of disability provided by disability studies have also, perhaps not surprisingly, had a minimal impact on sociology (Barton 1996). Not only does disability studies find itself diametrically opposed to the medical model of disability, it also finds it difficult to establish a relationship of mutual trust with medical sociology, mostly because the latter insists on conflating disability and sickness. Although medical sociologists have sought to critique the (bio)medical model of health, illness and the body (see Chapter 1), they have been reluctant to accept – and have even been hostile to – the idea of a social model of disability (see Bury 1996 and 1997):

> Although one of the most active sub-specialisms within sociology in both Europe and North America, medical sociology has consistently failed to respond to calls to rethink disability, except to dismiss the disabled people's movement as politically motivated and a threat to sociological values.
>
> (Barnes *et al.* 1999: 212)

Medical sociology in Britain has its origins in the functionalist and interactionist perspectives of US sociologists such as Talcott Parsons and Erving Goffman (Oliver 1996b). Parsons (1951) argued that 'good health' is the 'normal' state of being. Consequently, sickness and, by implication, impairment are a deviation from 'normality'. Subsequently, medical sociologists have placed much emphasis on analysing what they describe as the experience of 'chronic illness and disability' and its social ramifications, notably stigma management (Goffman 1968). Not only are chronic illness and disability assumed to be identical for analytical purposes, little attention is paid to the social relations that produce experiences of disability (Barnes 1998).

Early sociological studies of disability tended to underwrite rather than critique rehabilitation practice. An important influence was Safilios-Rothschild's (1970) notion of the 'rehabilitation role'. This position suggests that once a person with an impairment becomes aware of their condition they must 'accept it' and learn how to make the best of their lot (Oliver 1996b). People with impairments are not exempt from social expectations and responsibilities but must strive to adapt accordingly. Normality is the ideal against which success or failure is measured. Prostheses, for example, tend to mimic normal appearance and disabled people are expected to work with professionals on rehabilitation techniques and strategies in which their negative, pathological bodies are the objects of physical, emotional and moral re-formation.

This representation of the disabled body in rehabilitation practice has remained largely intact (Barnes *et al.* 1999). Medical sociologists have, however, shifted the debate. They argue that rehabilitation practice objectifies the body and consequently ignores the subjective experience of disabled people. From the perspective of disability studies, however, this critique of the 'rehabilitation role' is still trapped in the 'psychological imagination' (Oliver 1996b: 21). Although it shifts the issue from the soma to the domain of intersubjectivity, it still assumes that disability is an individual rather than a social problem.

Non-disabled medical sociologists have made assumptions about what it would be like to become disabled and imagined that it would require a difficult period of psychological adjustment. Phenomenological theories of psychological adjustment retain the assumption that disability is a personal tragedy (Oliver 1990) and therefore have no efficacy in challenging the pervasive negative cultural images of disability (see Pointon and Davis 1997) or the multiple barriers that disable the lives of people with impairments (Swain *et al.* 1993). Theories of disability, be they medical or sociological in origin, fail to consider the effects of discrimination and oppression.

This apolitical position is also evident in the view from medical sociology that treats disability as an issue that is best comprehended in terms of a biographical analysis of chronic illness. The passive broken body of the medical model remains an implicit assumption but is replaced as the substantive focus of analysis by the question of how individuals make sense of their 'disabled lives'. The problematic does not break with the apolitical micro-sociologies that dominated the analysis of disability in the 1960s and 1970s. It focuses on how people with impairments 'come to terms with' their disabled bodies, the meanings they assign to their bodily conditions and the ways in which these meanings permeate the negotiation of everyday life (Shakespeare and Watson 1997; Watson 1998). The contemporary interpretative approach to disability is reduced to the idea of 'biographical disruption' (Bury 1982, 1997), a term that represents disability as a sign of bodily chaos and emotional disorder, a cataclysm that corrupts an individual's sense of identity and self-worth (Charmaz 1983). It is, according to this logic, inevitably bad and sad to be disabled, and those who acquire or are born with an impairment had best spend their lives putting on a brave face and using every trick they can muster in order to appear as normal as possible. It is as if medical sociology is still in debt to the assumptions of 1960s 'labelling theory' which highlighted the intolerance of societal reaction to deviant bodies but could never quite escape the 'naturalism' that defined impairment as a 'primary deviance'.

Disability studies and the social model of disability

The confrontation with disablism in the medical and social sciences has resulted in the social model of disability. With respect to the meaning of disability, this model shifts its analytical gaze from the body to society. This position embodies a reversal of causality. Disability is conceptualized, therefore, not as an outcome of physical impairment but as an effect of social exclusion and discrimination. The longstanding imperative to cite bodily pathology as the ultimate cause of disability is challenged by this new discourse. It 'speaks' from the standpoint of disabled people and therefore voices an opinion that has, throughout modernity, been silenced by the paternalism of a non-disabled culture.

The social model challenges the assumption that disabled people cannot identify their own needs or act in their own interests.

Disability studies is founded on the work of Vic Finkelstein and Michael Oliver and it is linked to the rise of the disabled people's movement that was sparked by the UPIAS and the writings of Paul Hunt. Disability studies – particularly in the United Kingdom – rejects sociological approaches such as functionalism, interactionism and phenomenology but has considerable affinity with neo-Marxist, materialist theory. It suggests that disability is a product of the economic and social forces of capitalism (Oliver 1990) and that research should be concerned with illuminating the ways in which society disables people with impairments rather than with the impact of impairment on individual lives (Oliver 1992; Zarb 1992; Barnes and Mercer 1997). Watson (1998: 148) identifies the traditional discourse of disability that disability studies seeks to transcend:

> We already know that disabled people are stereotyped and that they lack cultural capital . . . consequently we do not need any more research into how disabled people cope with their impairment, the meaning that they ascribe to their impairment or how they organize their day-to-day lives.

Following the distinction between sex and gender that was significant for second-wave feminism in the 1970s, disability studies – in the process of arguing that inequality and exclusion were socially created – played down the importance of the body and embodied experience (Shakespeare 1994; Shakespeare and Watson 1995a, b). Just as feminist theory utilized the dualisms of nature and culture, sex and gender in the formation of a structural and generic analysis of sexism, so disability studies has utilized the binary of impairment and disability to shape its analysis of the oppression experienced by disabled people.

Since the 1970s a body of work that challenges the dominant view that disability is an individual problem of the body has emerged and matured. Finkelstein (1980) and Oliver (1990), deploying a historical materialist analysis, have argued that bodily pathology has been the defining characteristic of disability since the middle of the nineteenth century. The medicalization of disability was consequent upon the demand of the capitalist mode of production for 'unimpaired' labour power. Disabled people could not sell their labour because the bosses would not buy it. They were excluded from the labour market and, therefore, denied access to the means of survival. Whereas working men and women were oppressed by economic exploitation, disabled people were oppressed by denial of access to economic activity. Disability, therefore, is a historical product of capitalist social relations rather than an outcome of physical or mental impairment.

Vic Finkelstein, in his book *Attitudes and Disabled People* (1980), was the first disabled social scientist to establish a materialist framework for the analysis of disability. Finkelstein's central point is that disability is a product of the relationship between impairment and the 'ensemble of capitalist social relations'. The claim that disability is an individual and medical problem is, therefore, ideological. It arose at a specific historical moment – namely, the era of transition from feudalism to capitalism. For disabled people, this fundamental historical change meant a transition from 'integration' to 'segregation', from lives lived in the community to incarceration in institutions.

Before the social disruption of the processes of industrialization and urbanization that marked eighteenth- and nineteenth-century Western Europe, people with impairments were not segregated from the rest of society by incarceration or 'special treatment'. 'Cripples', as they were known, eked out a living at the lower end of the economic hierarchy by begging or by working on the land (Finkelstein 1980). 'Cripples', landless labourers, casual workers, those out of work and those with mental health problems formed a broad group of deprived and (sometimes) destitute people. There was – at least in early modernity – no elaborate system of demographic or medical classification to distinguish between the mass of mendicant and dispossessed peoples that had been pushed to the margins of society by the transition from feudalism to capitalism. However, the displacement of disabled people (among others) by the forces of capitalist development did not mean that hostility towards disabled people had its historical origins in this process. It was the specific historical form of discrimination that was new. Documentary evidence of negativity towards disabled people can be found in many religious texts, Greek philosophy and pre-Renaissance European art and drama (Barnes 1994). This discrimination was, however, relatively fragmented. Disabled people did not constitute a socially recognized group and they were not necessarily prevented from utilizing their labour power in the more flexible pattern of agrarian and cottage-based production.

However, this relative tolerance, which limited but did not exclude disabled people from economic activity, ended with the dawn of the Industrial Revolution and the development of new techniques and processes of production (Finkelstein 1980). In the newly mechanized world where the rhythm of work was dictated by the machine rather than the worker, the labour power of people with impairments became surplus to requirements (Barnes *et al.* 1999). There was no place for disabled people in the mills and the factories. Deprived of access to the (dark, satanic) places of subsistence and survival, disabled people joined the growing ranks of itinerants and became a 'social problem'. Forced into idleness, they became categorized as 'unproductive' and consequently burdensome. These processes served to exacerbate traditional fears and prejudices which in turn legitimated the systematic exclusion and segregation of disabled people (Barnes 1994). Severed from the mainstream of social life and gradually identified as a population who could be distinguished by their physical and intellectual 'deficits' or 'abnormalities', disabled people found themselves increasingly under the jurisdiction of medical science. As Ryan and Thomas

(1980: 101) have argued: 'The asylums of the nineteenth century were . . . as much the result of far-reaching changes in work and family life, and corresponding methods of containing the poor, as they were the inspiration of philanthropists and scientists.'

The growing ranks of the medical profession were given the task of policing those who had been constituted as disabled, and therefore unemployable, by the vicissitudes of a system in which survival depended on the marketability of one's physical labour. Marginalized by (labour) market forces, disabled people were 'rounded up' and incarcerated in medical institutions. Once 'inside' they were constituted as objects of care that had been rescued from destitution. These places were far from benevolent. They were stark warehouses with strict prison-like regimes, and their inmates were defined as the 'deserving' recipients of bourgeois philanthropy or miserly forms of state assistance. The Victorian philanthropic imagination differentiated between those who were unable to work and therefore 'deserving' of support and charity and the 'undeserving' – those who resisted the ethical imperative to work out of pure idleness (Oliver 1990). This dichotomous system of moral classification was important in constituting disabled people as a distinct group within the generic mass of poor people whose vast and visible numbers haunted the landscape of early industrial capitalism. The concepts of 'ability' and 'disability' as applied to human populations emerged, therefore, from the bourgeois value system that judged human worth in terms of an individual's capacity for and willingness to work. Impaired bodies might be willing, but they were not able. They were without use and therefore, in a society that prized utility, a problem. Formally, the Victorian – or should it be Dickensian – solution to (non-criminal) deviancy was sanctuary, but in practice this was a euphemism for segregation and incarceration.

The incarceration of people with impairments continued throughout the nineteenth century and the first half of the twentieth century. The rise of scientific medicine during this period and its success in medicalizing physical and mental life gave doctors the authority not only to command the spaces of incarceration (Finkelstein 1980; Barnes *et al.* 1999) but also the bodies that inhabited them. As medicine began to consolidate its raison d'être as a heroic pursuit, the rationale of 'care' gave way to 'cure' and disabled bodies became objects of scientific experimentation – guinea-pigs in the service of medical progress. A new logic entered the spaces in which disabled people were confined. If people with impairments were destitute because their bodies were not commensurate with the demands of the factory floor, then their bodies should be repaired. If the body was a machine with interconnecting parts and functions, then the impaired body was a faulty machine. If its parts did not work correctly, it was for this reason that it was disabled. The logic of medical reductionism arrived at the simple conclusion that impairment was the cause of disability. The unfit could be made 'fit', for the world of work, by medical treatment.

The 'surplus to value' could be made valuable and productive. Medical logic had adjusted itself perfectly to the cultural logic of industrial capitalism and secured a place for itself in the system as the principal agency charged with the restoration of impaired labour power. The success of the science of rehabilitation rested on the promise that it would bear economic fruit. Disability became a sickness and scientific medicine became the outstanding player in the welfare team that delivered services for the 'therapeutic state', which has been described as the place of 'novel and polarized conceptions of normal and abnormal, sane and insane, healthy and sick' (Barnes *et al.* 1999: 19).

Michael Oliver's monograph, *The Politics of Disablement* (1990), takes this materialist analysis further. Anthropological studies show that the perception of disability as an individual health problem is not universal. Rather, it is related to the socioeconomic environment and to the dominant values of specific societies (see Ingstad and Whyte 1995). The hegemony of the individual model of disability is a product of the social relations of capitalist production and the ideology of individualism that helps sustain it. Oliver (1990: xii) argues that 'disability is ultimately produced by the functional needs of capital for a particular kind of work force'. Individualism is the organic or core ideology of capitalism. The system requires individuals to sell their labour in a free market and therefore prioritizes individual biophysical fitness. It expects disabled people to make 'adjustments' – often with the assistance of medicine – that will maximize their labour power as individuals.

Individualism, the core ideology of capitalism, is complemented by peripheral ideologies that flesh out the dominant meaning of disability. These are medicalization and personal tragedy theory. They construct disability as, respectively, an individual health problem and as an individual existential crisis which requires a charitable response (Oliver 1990). The idea of disability as a personal tragedy and individual medical problem is made possible by the somatic dichotomy that distinguishes between normal and abnormal bodies. This dichotomy is, itself, closely related to the value placed on the productivity of the labouring body (Oliver 1990). Modern biomedicine has therefore developed a system for categorizing individuals as either 'able-bodied' and productive or as disabled and unproductive. As Oliver (1990: 46) states, 'The core (organic) ideology of individualism gives rise to the ideological construction of the disabled individual as the antithesis of able-bodiedness and able-mindedness, and the medicalization of disability as a particular kind of problem.'

The cultural stereotype that conceives of disability as a medical problem and a personal tragedy is reproduced by traditional and dominant academic representations of disability (Oliver 1990 and 1996a). It is the task of the social model of disability to critique and challenge the economic, social and cultural constitution of disability as the epitome of somatic 'alterity'. The social model, therefore, does not represent disability as a personal limitation of the body or an unfortunate twist of fate, but as a situation produced by a social and spatial environment that fails to acknowledge the needs and rights of people with impairments. For the social model, impairment is a corporeal concept and disability a social product. The latter arises as a consequence of social relations rather than corporeal deficit. The idea of 'able-bodiedness' is also a product of these social relations. Disability studies and the disabled people's movement, therefore, understand disability in terms diametrically opposed to dominant social representations, including the 'normalizing' sciences of medicine and rehabilitation. Disability studies seeks to challenge the myth of 'biophysical normality' and to expose the barriers that exclude and marginalize disabled people. However, although this agenda defines disability in structural terms as a form of social oppression (Abberley 1987), it ignores a sociological consideration of impairment and the body (Hughes 1999).

Towards a sociology of impairment

The second section of this chapter focused on the irony that it was disability studies rather than sociology that established disability as a social and sociological category. The third section mapped out the materialist and structuralist position that formed the backbone of the specific nature of this category. A major strength of the social model's structural account lay in its efficacy as a tool that could be used to demedicalize and denaturalize disability. This was of considerable political importance, because, as Tom Shakespeare (1992: 40) has argued, 'to mention biology, to admit pain, to confront our impairments, has been to risk the oppressors seizing on evidence that disability is really about physical limitation after all'. For disability studies – as it matured and developed in the 1980s and early 1990s – impairment was a taboo subject. During the same period, the social model was received enthusiastically by many disabled people and even some 'welfare professionals'. It is not yet the 'new orthodoxy' but it is now well quoted as a strong contestant in the struggle to delineate the meaning of disability. Yet, despite its success, disabled people have begun to question the adequacy of the explanatory power of the social model, largely because it is silent on the question of impairment. Part of the problem lies with the displacement, if not complete effacement, of the social and political aspects of embodiment. The social model of disability denies the embodied experiences of pain and affliction that are an integral part of the lives of many people with impairments (Morris 1991; Crow 1996). Furthermore, if disability studies neglected social and political accounts of impairment and the body, it would find itself adrift with respect to some of the most telling debates of the age. In 'somatic society', as Terrence Turner (1994: 27) has noted by way of the following attenuated but compelling list, the 'biological' and the sociopolitical are locked into one another:

The body or embodied subject is the object of seduction by advertising, interpellation by semiotically loaded commodities, torture
by a broad spectrum of political regimes, bitter conflicts over
reproductive life and health care, struggles for the revaluation of
alternate sexual identities, threats from new epidemic diseases,
and the object of new technologies permitting the alteration of
physical attributes hitherto accepted as naturally determined,
including cosmetic surgery, asexual and extra-sexual fertilization,
multiple forms of intervention in the biological process of reproduction and modification of genetic traits and the artificial pro-
longation or curtailment of the span of life itself.

The challenge to the radical separation of impairment and disability
came not only from the experience of disabled people themselves and
the demands of a world in which 'biopolitics' is omnipresent, but also
from the post-Cartesian sensibilities of the contemporary intelligentsia.
Michel Foucault has argued, on countless occasions, that the body has
a history and is a social construction. Donna Haraway (1991: 10) –
with more than a nod to a Marxist anthropology of the body – argued
that, 'Neither our personal bodies nor our social bodies may be seen
as natural in the sense of existing outside the self-creating process of
human labour.' A similar argument is explained with commendable
clarity in the following passage:

Scholars have only recently discovered that the human body itself
has a history. Not only has it been perceived, interpreted and
represented differently in different epochs, but it has also been
lived differently, brought into being within widely dissimilar
material cultures, subjected to various technologies and means of
control and incorporated into different rhythms of production
and consumption, pleasure and pain.

(Gallacher and Laqueur 1987: vii)

In the 1980s and early 1990s, disability studies stood outside these
debates. Second-wave feminism was at the heart of them because
it had revised the view that sex and gender belonged to mutually
exclusive ontological domains. If new theoretical departures and
social developments could convince that 'sex' was not a biological
fact of life but a social construction, then impairment was ripe for
the same theoretical treatment (Shakespeare 1992; Shakespeare and
Watson 1995a, b). 'Insiders' in the disability movement began to pay
more sustained attention to the convincing argument that social and
physical 'difference' in a common generic identity produced variations
in the experience of oppression that could not be glossed over. Debates
about how the experience of disability varied with respect to class,
gender, race and sexuality spilled over into impairment.

As the debate began to develop, it became fairly clear that the social
model had posited a body devoid of any historical or social substance.

In so doing, it had, in fact, conceded impairment to medicine. 'There is a powerful convergence between biomedicine and the social model of disability with respect to the body. Both treat it as a pre-social, inert, physical object, as discrete, palpable and separate from the self' (Hughes and Paterson 1997: 329). Frank (1990: 136), in an important contribution to the sociology of the body, had argued that 'our capacity to experience the body directly or theorise it indirectly, is inextricably medicalized'. This, ironically, was an argument that could be applied to the way in which the social model had defined impairment. 'Lacking part or all of a limb, or having a defective limb, organism or mechanism of the body' (UPIAS 1976: 3) is the usual definition quoted by proponents of the social model. This is, of course, a definition that would not look out of place in any medical dictionary. This implies that although medicine has an ideological view of disability, it is wholly neutral and objective with respect to impairment. The way to avoid this contradiction is to treat impairment, like disability, as a cultural construct and to admit to the possibility of a sociology or social model of impairment. In disability studies this argument has not yet been won, but there is a growing body of research that accepts that the somatic, cultural and linguistic turns provide a theoretical context in which the social aspects of impairment and the embodied aspects of disability can be fruitfully delineated (L. Davis 1995; Shakespeare and Watson 1995a, b; Wendell 1996; Hughes and Paterson 1997; Corker 1999; Corker and French 1999; Hughes 1999; Paterson and Hughes 1999).

Conclusion

The inability to generate an adequate theory of disability has been one of the more spectacular failures of modern sociological research. When it comes to impairment and disability, medical sociology is still trapped in a residual naturalism, and although the sociology of the body has escaped that mire it still shows few signs of interest in disability. To conceptualize disability apolitically on the level of inter-subjective experience or in terms of stigma has had some descriptive value and it goes down well in liberal circles where a 'sociology of the underdog' has always had some cachet (Abberley 1999; Hughes 1999). But one can hardly expect disabled people to get too excited about a sociological tradition that understands impairment as a 'primary deviance' and disability as the secondary, negative social reaction to it. It promotes the view that non-disabled people should be more charitable to and tolerable of their disabled counterparts, but it is hardly likely to bring down the countless barriers to social participation that perpetually invalidate disabled people's lives. It might go some way to modifying prejudicial attitudes but it is little more than superfluous with respect to institutional discrimination. The more that disabled people have refused to be constituted by the voice, vision and organizational ineptitude of non-disabled people, the more they have preferred to forgo sociological civility and campaign for civil rights.

It is hardly surprising, therefore, that in the past 20 years disabled people have 'preferred to reinterpret their collective experiences in terms of structural notions of discrimination and oppression rather than interpersonal ones of stigma and stigmatization' (Oliver 1990: 68). This reinterpretation, which drew heavily on Marxist sociology, was the inspiration not of sociology itself, but of disability studies. In this guise, disability studies became the theoretical expression of the disabled people's movement and set about transforming the meaning of disability from a bodily condition to a site of social oppression. Disability studies – as it struggles with contemporary questions of identity and embodiment – continues to borrow heavily from sociology, particularly in its contemporary 'post-Cartesian' forms. In light of the collapse of the distinction between nature and culture, disability studies has had to revisit the watertight distinction between impairment and disability which constituted its founding dichotomy. A more compelling reason, however, for theoretical re-evaluation arose from the practice of adopting a politics of pride. If disability was a form of social oppression, one could hardly be proud to be oppressed. Pride, on the contrary, was to be found in a celebration of physical being – its difference, its potential, its beauty and its integrity. Disability pride is a positive, collective, aesthetic expression of self-recognition that constitutes a 'great refusal' to accept discrimination and second-class citizenship.

Further reading

Understanding Disability: From Theory to Practice (1996a) by Mike Oliver is a useful starting point. This book is a personal journey of exploration by a disabled person who has contributed immeasurably to disability studies, and an interesting attempt to progress disability theory. The best account of the 'social model of disability' as well as the most penetrating Marxist critique of the individual or medical model can be found in Mike Oliver's influential monograph, *The Politics of Disablement* (1990). For an overview of key developments in disability studies over the past 10–15 years, the most appropriate point of reference is Len Barton and Mike Oliver's edited collection *Disability Studies: Past, Present and Future* (1997). The collection contains seminal articles from the journal *Disability & Society*. This journal is, in itself, a rich source of insight and debate and is dominated by articles that are written from a 'social model' perspective. Disability studies is a multidisciplinary approach and this fact is well represented in Tom Shakespeare's edited anthology *The Disability Reader: Social Science Perspectives* (1998). This volume has a US 'equivalent' which – unlike

Shakespeare's volume – has few transparent ties to disabled people's struggles, and is far less dependent on the materialist social model but is more conscious of the cultural turn. It is edited by Leonard Davis (1997) and entitled *The Disability Studies Reader*. Of texts devoted to the sociology of disability Len Barton's edited volume *Disability and Society: Emerging Issues and Insights* (1996) is useful. So too is the very digestible co-authored text by Colin Barnes, Geof Mercer and Tom Shakespeare entitled *Exploring Disability: A Sociological Introduction* (1999). The gulf between disability studies and medical sociology regarding their conceptions of illness, impairment and disability is traversed by Colin Barnes and Geof Mercer's edited collection *Exploring the Divide: Illness and Disability* (1996). For a feminist perspective on disability, check out Jenny Morris' *Pride against Prejudice: Transforming Attitudes to Disability* (1991) and *Encounters with Strangers: Feminism and Disability* (1996). These texts raised important criticisms about disability studies' disembodied view of disability which have been taken forward by Marian Corker and Sally French (1999) in *Disability Discourse*.

CHAPTER 3

Consumer bodies

ELIZABETH JAGGER

Introduction

One of the broad social changes that has brought the body into prominence in sociology has been the growth of a 'consumer culture'.
Although the origins of 'modern consumption' practices have a longer
history in different locations (Miller *et al.* 1998), several major social
transformations taking place throughout the twentieth century had
firmly established the foundations of a 'consumer culture' by the postwar period. These include the rise of the media and advertising (Ewen
1976; Ewen and Ewen 1982), the decline of heavy manufacturing
industries and the growth in service sector industries. Such changes
have been associated with the decline of the traditional worker,
together with the growing salience of lifestyles based on leisure and
consumption activities (Turner 1991). According to Turner (1991),
the shortening of the working week, compulsory retirement and the
valorization of sport and recreation have meant that conventional
wisdom concerning the virtues of hard work have now been over-
shadowed by an emphasis on consumption, hedonism and play. In
effect, the work ethic has been replaced by a consumption ethic
(Bell 1976; Bauman 1998). Such transformations have brought questions of the self to the forefront of the political, economic and social
stage. According to Tomlinson (1990), sources of identity and a sense
of self are derived less from work and production than from consumption and leisure. As Rose (1989: 102) has pointed out:

> The primary economic image offered to the modern citizen is not
> that of the producer but of the consumer. Through consumption

we are urged to shape our lives by the use of our purchasing power. We are obliged to make our lives meaningful by selecting our personal lifestyle from those offered to us in advertising, soap operas, and films, to make sense of our existence by exercising our freedom to choose in a market in which one simultaneously purchases products and services, and assembles, manages, and markets oneself.

Moreover, it can be argued that in consumer culture the self is inextricably bound up with the body. According to Shilling (1993), with the decline of religious authority and its certainties, the progressive privatization of meaning and a loss of faith in grand political narratives, the physical body seems to provide a firm foundation for the construction and affirmation of identity. In Featherstone's (1991a) phrase, the body has become the 'visible carrier of the self'.

This chapter argues that the body plays a mediating role between consumer activities and the cultural constitution of the self. For the body not only acts as a medium through which messages about self-identity are transmitted but is also a key site for the marking of difference (Shilling 1993). The development of this argument, however, requires some explanation of the concepts it deploys.

'Consumption' is used throughout the chapter to refer to the purchase and use of goods, leisure activities and services such as shopping for clothes, dining out and engaging in fitness regimes or other bodily projects. Consumption is motivated by consumerism – the ideology pervading modern capitalism that prioritizes the production, sale and acquisition of consumer goods and services. The term 'consumer culture', however, refers to the norms and values of a consumer society and points not only to the importance of cultural goods as commodities but also to the way in which most cultural activities are now mediated through consumption (Featherstone 1991b). Specifically, it draws attention to the symbolic aspect of goods and the way in which they are used as communicators (Featherstone 1991b). In short, cultural goods are consumed not merely for their use-value (their material utility), but for their sign value (for what they signify). Importantly, symbolic consumption is fundamental to the process by which modern individuals create and display their identities. By 'identity' is meant a sense of who we are, and how we relate to others and to the cultural and social context in which we live. 'Identity', according to Woodward (1997), is concerned with the extent to which we are the same as or different from others. Cultural goods are of salience here because they are deployed in strategies of social distinction (Bourdieu 1984). That is, commodities are used not only to convey messages about the self, but also to establish communality with some individuals or groups and to demarcate difference from others.

The main theme of the chapter is thus to explore the interconnections between consumption, identity and the body, drawing on the work of commentators who, in diverse ways, have addressed these links. Although most authors agree that symbolic consumption is central to the constitution of self-identity, there are some theoretical disagreements between writers as to how this link can be explained and understood. For example, writers such as Bourdieu (1984) continue to emphasize rigidly defined class-based identities whereas postmodern writers see identities as being dynamic, plural and derived from a multiplicity of sources. Thus, whereas for Bourdieu we consume according to who we are (consumer choices are inscribed on the body establishing social differences), for postmodern theorists we become what we consume (the body is saturated with cultural signs with no fixed referents, producing multiple, shifting identities) (Jameson 1985; Baudrillard 1988b).

It can be argued, however, that most of those theorists mentioned above have frequently paid insufficient attention to gender in their discussions of identity formation and re-formation. Given that access to cultural resources is not equally available to men and women in consumer culture, it has been argued that reflexive self-fashioning (Giddens 1991) is more problematic for women (Lury 1996). Women, for instance, experience a relative lack of control in terms of self-definition. Thus the constraints and insecurities women confront in claiming ownership of their feminine subjectivity are explored and exemplified here through a discussion of a specific bodily project – body building. As Benson (1997) has pointed out, this is one arena in which women seek to rewrite the self by rewriting the body, engaging in a conscious process of bodily transformation.

Before this argument is elaborated on in any detail, however, section one of the chapter outlines briefly the historical emergence of consumer culture and its contemporary salient features; section two discusses the work of authors who have sought to explain the links between consumption and identity; and this is followed by an extension of their arguments in relation to the body in section three. Section four considers the contributions of feminists to these debates; and finally the chapter ends with a discussion of body building.

The emergence of a consumer culture

The salient features and attributes of contemporary consumer culture can be traced back to a range of developments that provided the foundations for its emergence. In exploring these historical conditions, different authors have identified diverse contexts over a long period. Although authors such as Schama (1987) have traced its origins to the seventeenth century in the Netherlands and McKendrick *et al.* (1982) and Porter (1990) to the eighteenth century in England, other writers such as Williams (1982) and Miller (1981) have located these in the nineteenth century for France and the USA. Ewen (1976) and Susman (1982), however, emphasize that it was not until the years between the First and Second World Wars in the USA and Britain that consumer culture became fully established. Most writers agree, however, that it developed initially in the middle classes and gradually spread to the working classes. According to Alt (1976), mass consumption was the necessary 'other' of mass production. As McKendrick *et al.* (1982) have pointed out, 'The consumer revolution was the necessary analogue to the industrial revolution, the necessary convulsion on the demand side of the equation to match the convulsion on the supply side' (1982: 9). Productive capacities had been increased dramatically in the late nineteenth century by the development of scientific management and the introduction of assembly-line production and Fordist techniques of work organization (see Chapter 6 of this volume). Demand was stimulated by improvements in real wages, the introduction of consumer credit and the instalment plan. Standardized goods became available to wider markets with the development of fast and efficient railway networks (as well as sea and road transport systems) linking large industrial cities. In particular, the new era of consumer culture was inaugurated by, and institutionalized in, the rise of the department store (Chaney 1983) where the profusion of goods on display offered new freedoms and opportunities for consumer indulgence. City centres became places of extravagant entertainment with their numerous eating places, bars and saloons, and elaborate theatres (Chaney 1996). Customers were seduced by new forms of display using plate glass windows, electric lighting and all the resources of architectural spectacle in the transformation of public space (Bronner 1989).

The new industrial situation with its proliferation of cheap mass-produced goods, however, needed what Ewen (1976: 32) calls 'a continually responsive consumer market'. Whereas previously consumers demanded reliable goods, now manufacturers needed reliable consumers (Corrigan 1996). Hence, workers who had previously been socialized into the puritan values of thrift, denial, hard work, sobriety and moderation, had to be 're-educated' to appreciate values that extolled the virtues of unbridled consumption, to espouse a 'new discourse centred around the hedonistic lifestyle entailing new needs and desires' (Featherstone 1991a: 172). By the 1920s, new ideals and norms of behaviour were publicized by the nascent media of motion pictures, mass spectator sport, the tabloid press, mass circulation magazines, radio, the fashion and cosmetic industries and, above all, through advertising. Advertising became one of the main conduits for conveying cultural values, creating new markets for goods and stimulating fresh buying habits. As Featherstone (1991a) has pointed out, advertising became the guardian of the new morality, encouraging individuals to take part in the consumption of commodities previously restricted to the upper classes, albeit in modified forms. Advertising celebrated the new consumption ethic, advocating the values of self-expression, living for the moment, the exotica of far-away places, freedom from social obligations and the cultivation of style (Featherstone

1991a). It attached images of youth, beauty, luxury and romance to even the most mundane of products, making them desirable to the general population. It did this by using what Baudrillard (1975) has called the 'floating signifier' effect. For Baudrillard (1975) one of the immanent features of consumer culture is the dominance of the exchange-value of commodities (the price for which goods can be sold in the marketplace), which has erased their original use-value (their purpose or utility) to such an extent that they are now free to take on any meaning depending on their position in a system of signifiers that is self-referential. In other words, signifiers, like television advertisements, 'float' freely with only the loosest connection to actual objects. With the advent of the commodity as sign, consumer goods became attractive for their symbolism – for the imagery surrounding them and what this might 'say' about the person who buys or uses them. It is the difference between buying designer jeans and a chain store version; the former would be bought in preference to the latter because of the style or social status associated with them.

A focus on the allure of goods, however, was not the only strategy that advertising deployed in generating demand and inducing consumers to buy. It also aimed to produce a specific kind of consumer – one who would be particularly receptive to its message. One way it did this was to present individuals as the object of continual scrutiny by others (Ewen 1976). According to Ewen (1976), the intention was that the consumer's critical functions should be turned away from the product and towards him or her self. Advertisements were often designed to make people feel ashamed of themselves and inadequate. As Featherstone (1991a) has pointed out, they created a climate in which individuals were made to feel emotionally vulnerable and so were encouraged to monitor themselves constantly for any imperfections that could no longer be construed as natural or unavoidable. The message was, therefore, that there was always room for self-improvement through the purchase and use of a vast array of consumer goods (Featherstone 1991a).

Consumer culture was firmly established by the end of the Second World War, since when it has drawn more and more people into a hectic and ever-expanding cycle of consumption. The common assumption of the 1920s that mass production would lead to a parallel growth in free time or leisure has proved to be largely illusory (Cross 1993). Instead, it has led to the creation of a 'harried leisure class' of consumers (Cross 1993). As Featherstone (1991a) has pointed out, the progressive expansion of the market has brought increasing areas of social life within its trajectory, advocating the need for commodities not only in the domestic sphere but also in leisure activities. As hobbies have become increasingly dependent on the purchase of commodities, they require systematic planning and an ever-increasing expenditure of time on their organization. Consumer durables themselves need continual maintenance which leads invariably to the need for further purchases, shopping for which takes time and organization, thus further eating into free time (Featherstone 1991a). In short, individuals now have to work much harder at being consumers, in what Cross (1993) has described as a 'work-and-spend' culture. In documenting the qualities that consumer culture demands of its members, Bauman (1998) points out that consumers are now required to be energetic, alert, impetuous, restive, excitable, sensation-seeking and passionate. Although eager to make new choices from the panoply of goods displayed, they must also be equally susceptible to losing interest, for it is the volatility of their engagement that matters. A new vocabulary of consumption, displaying these novel attitudes, has entered everyday discourse and is evident in phrases such as 'to die for', in magazines where 'must haves' now describes the latest articles for sale (for example the *Sunday Times* magazine carries a regular column headed 'Most Wanted: this week's object of desire'), and in the titles of television programmes such as *She's Gotta Have It*. Consumption, then, is far from being simply about the satisfaction of fixed needs; it is about desires and dreams, albeit that no desire should be considered ultimate. As Bauman (1998) has pointed out, in shortening the time and space between desire and consummation, consumer culture has taken the waiting out of wanting and the wanting out of waiting. Hence, endless desire and longing as opposed to need and a utilitarian attitude now fuels the consumer game. Importantly for the argument here, it is desire for the sign, not the commodity itself, that links consumption to the constitution of self-identity.

Consumption and identity

It was argued earlier that although it is generally acknowledged that modern identities are constructed through symbolic consumption, contemporary cultural theorists have different views on how this relationship can be explained. Bourdieu's (1984) interest in this is part of his general concern with social reproduction and the reproduction of class relations in particular. For Bourdieu identities are located in relatively stable and fixed social class positions which determine particular constellations of consumption preferences in any social field such as art, sport, diet, furnishings, music and so forth. Thus, in his view, taste in cultural goods operates as a marker of class identity. Because consumption choices involve discriminatory judgements of taste, they simultaneously render visible to others an individual's or social group's own particular discriminatory capacities. As Bourdieu has expressed it, taste classifies the classifier. To explain the social determinants of taste that characterize a particular class or class fraction, Bourdieu introduces the notion of 'habitus'. By 'habitus' Bourdieu is referring to a set of unconscious dispositions that organize an individual's capacity to act, to classify and to make sense of social experience. It is manifest in an individual's taken-for-granted assumptions about the appropriateness and validity of his or her taste in cultural goods and practices. To put it simply, a person or group's 'habitus' is what makes their good taste (or absence of it) seem to be 'natural'. The application of this set of classificatory principles as distinctive modes of cultural consumption is thus recognized as a sign of taste or the lack of it. As Featherstone has pointed out:

> The modern individual within consumer culture is made conscious that he speaks not only with his clothes, but with his home, furnishings, decoration, car and other activities which are to be read and classified in terms of the presence and absence of taste.
> (Featherstone 1991b: 86)

Thus, according to Bourdieu (1984), symbolic consumption is an ideal weapon in strategies of distinction. Cultural goods are deployed to demarcate boundaries between some individuals or social groups and to establish communality with others. In the general struggle for dominance, different classes try to impose their own habitus on others, to legitimate their own tastes. However, for Bourdieu (1984) it is not merely the purchase of cultural goods that is important, but the manner of using them. Given that different class groups have differing amounts of, and access to, 'cultural capital' – the sedimented knowledge and competence to make judgements of taste acquired through expenditure of time and money on such unproductive matters (Corrigan 1996) – each act of consumption reproduces social differences.

Rather than seeing identity as rigidly defined in terms of class, however, postmodern writers have tended to introduce notions of fluidity and plurality into their formulations. From a postmodern perspective, identities are no longer received automatically through the rituals and social practices of the traditional order, but are constituted through individual marketplace decisions. As Bauman has pointed out in commenting on the cultural changes in forms and sources of identities in the passage from a 'producer' to a 'consumer' society, 'The roads to self-identity, to a place in society, to a life in a form recognizable as that of meaningful living, all require daily visits to the market place' (Bauman 1998: 26). In effect, it is argued, we become what we consume. According to postmodern theorists, as the pace of life has accelerated and as society has become more open, so releasing individuals from the constraints of traditional social positions, identities have become more unstable, fragile and subject to change. By providing a series of 'expert knowledges', for instance in relation to lifestyle, health, fashion and beauty, consumer culture is understood from a postmodern perspective to have contributed to an increasingly reflexive understanding of the self, an awareness that identity is chosen and constructed (Giddens 1991; Kellner 1995). As Giddens (1991) has pointed out, the self in 'late modernity' has become a reflexive project; it is created (and re-created) through a plurality of consumer choices and lifestyle decisions. In his view, individuals can now draw on a wide repertoire

of symbolic goods with which to fashion and display their own identities. According to Featherstone (1991a), the 'new heroes' of consumer
culture display their individuality in the particular way they assemble
goods, clothes, practices and appearances and design them together
into a lifestyle.

However, whereas Giddens tends to see the self as a unitary, self-
regulated attainment (Turner 1992), other authors have suggested that
the self has a plurality of identities constituted in diverse contexts
and often dependent on consumer-defined figurations. Writers such
as Jameson (1985) and Baudrillard (1988b), for example, have argued
that the self-constituting subject is now fragmentary and inherently
unstable. Indeed, Baudrillard (1988b) has even gone so far as to argue
that the subject has now disappeared. As culture becomes increasingly
fragmented, without depth, substantiality and coherence, an individual's sense of identity is understood to break down, resulting in a
'decentred self'. The overload of information and the overproduction
of signs lead to the destabilization of identity. The surfeit of signs and
images produced by consumerism and television has erased the distinction between the real and the imaginary (Baudrillard 1983). Hence
this simulational world is understood to provide few fixed reference
points for self-constituting subjects. Instead, they engage in an endless,
superficial play with signs and images, producing multiple and shifting identities. In other words, individuals use commodities and their
random, open-ended meanings to continually reinvent themselves.
Modern selves, then – delighting in the notion that signs are opaque,
meaningless and thus cannot be decoded – reject or parody traditional
status games. From a postmodern perspective, in this context of
'cultural disorder' with its 'death of the social' and 'loss of the real'
(Baudrillard 1983), the relatively stable sets of classificatory principles
(habitus) that are socially recognizable and function to demarcate
boundaries between groups are held to disappear (Featherstone 1991b).
No longer are there any universally agreed on criteria for judgements of cultural taste; indeed, from a postmodern perspective there
are understood to be no fixed status or age groups or social classes as
such.

For Jameson and Baudrillard, therefore, although identities are constructed through the consumption of signs, they are not reducible to
class in the manner indicated by Bourdieu. Instead anyone can be
anyone – as long as they have the means to participate in consumption.

Consumption, identity and the body

It was argued earlier that in consumer culture self-identity is inextricably bound up with the body and its surfaces. Although most commentators agree that the consumer self is an embodied self, there is
some variation between writers in the extent to which this notion

has been discussed in any detail. For instance, although Giddens (1991) recognizes that the consumer body is implicated in modern identities, because his main concern is with the reflexive self he does not deal with the embodied self in any great depth. Similarly, the postmodern body, although conceptualized as a fragmented body untrammelled by considerations of class, remains largely undeveloped in the theoretical formulations of Jameson (1985) and Baudrillard (1983). According to these authors, it is the image of the body rather than the body as such that is central to identity. The body is seen as being saturated with cultural signs or as becoming merely a series of cultural quotations. Thus, in this view, modern individuals collapse into their images and their self-identity becomes free floating. Indeed, Baudrillard (1988b) goes so far as to argue that since signs have no referents and do not signify anything outside themselves, rather than people using objects to articulate differences between themselves, individuals have become merely the vehicles for expressing differences between objects. According to this view, not only do individual identities dissolve into a 'glutinous mass', but the body itself disappears from the analysis (Frank 1991).

Hence, although it will be suggested that his account might be problematic, it is nevertheless the work of Bourdieu that has made one of the most significant contributions to an understanding of the links between consumption, identity and the body. In contrast to postmodern approaches where the body is in effect dematerialized, for Bourdieu the body is the materialization of class taste. The body bears the imprint of the consumption practices of various social classes. As indicated earlier, these consumption choices are dependent on the habitus of particular classes or class fractions. It should be pointed out here, however, that habitus does not simply operate at the level of everyday knowledgeability or competences, but, according to Bourdieu, is embodied – literally. That is, it is made manifest in body size, shape and weight, posture, demeanour, ways of walking, eating and drinking, and sense of ease with one's body; even in the amount of social space a person feels entitled to occupy. Each class or class fraction, then, has a clearly identifiable relationship with its body, which results in the production of distinct bodily forms. For instance, the working class have an instrumental relationship with their body whereas the middle class are more concerned with their body's appearance and intrinsic functioning. Hence the former tend to engage in weight lifting, producing bodies that exhibit strength, whereas the latter are more likely to choose jogging, producing a fit, slim body. For Bourdieu, the body is a form of physical capital that can also be converted to attain other forms of capital – economic, social and cultural. The possibilities for conversion, however, have differing degrees of opportunity and risk attached, based on class belonging. Importantly, according to Bourdieu, some bodily forms are deemed to have a higher symbolic value than others. The symbolic values attached to particular bodily forms thus have implications for an individual's sense of identity and the way in which the body is a site of struggle in strategies of distinction – a site for the marking of difference. Central to this struggle for distinction is the capacity of the dominant group to define their own bodies as superior, as 'valuable bodies'.

In contemporary consumer culture, however, there are potential difficulties in the imposition of a single hegemonic classificatory scheme throughout society (Shilling 1993). As Featherstone (1991b) has pointed out, the globalization and circulation of consumer 'lifestyle' commodities may threaten the readability of those signs deployed by the dominant group to signal their elite physical capital. For instance, it is not uncommon in contemporary society for working-class people to save for and acquire designer clothes and household furnishings. In Featherstone's view, even if it is still possible to read status differences from bodily dispositions and consumption choices, it is obvious that the game is much more complex now. It should be pointed out, however, that although there has been some discussion of class in relation to the body and consumption, most of these writers have tended to neglect the significance of gender and hence the particularities of women's embodied experiences.

Gender, consumption and the body

The relationship between gender, the body and consumer culture has received relatively little attention in sociology. Although many of the 'new body theorists' acknowledge the influence of feminism as a political movement on the emergence of the body as a topic, actual feminist scholarship on the body is notably absent from their accounts (Shilling 1993 and 1997 are exceptions). Similarly, writers on consumer culture have assumed that modern selves in search of their identity projects experience this culture in a homogeneous and universal manner without any consideration being given to gender or other socially constructed differences. These writers thus tend to imply that men and women have the same capacities to define and constitute their own embodied identities. For example, authors such as Giddens and Featherstone frequently assume that cultural resources are equally available to men and women when reflexively fashioning their own identities. But as Lury (1996) has pointed out, women in general do not necessarily have the same capacities to claim ownership of their identities as men, given that these are typically more a reflection of male fantasies and expectations than an expression of their own sense of self. According to Tyler and Abbott (1998), Giddens' understanding of the body as an integral element of 'the reflexive project of the self' (Giddens 1991: 219) seriously underestimates the extent to which women's bodies as 'projects' continue to be more reflective of patriarchal norms and instrumentally imposed aesthetic codes of 'femininity' than expressions of a self-determined individuality.

It can be argued therefore that a feminist scholarship on the body in consumer society is a welcome corrective to the masculinist character of these approaches. In feminist writings on the consumer body, however, two separate, and potentially opposing, strands are identifiable. In the first strand, women are located as the objects of consumption and consumerism; the relationship between femininity, consumption and the body is seen as oppressive to women. In the second strand, by contrast, women are situated as the subjects of consumption and consumerism, with authors suggesting that women are well able to resist, challenge or reappropriate cultural goods and practices in order to fashion their own subjectivity. However, as will be suggested, women's relationship to consumer culture is more complex than either of these perspectives imply, to the extent that women are simultaneously the objects and subjects of consumption.

As K. Davis (1997a) has pointed out, feminists have taken domination, difference and subversion as their starting point for understanding the conditions and experiences of embodiment in consumer culture. Initially, however, feminist work on the body invariably linked women's embodied experiences to practices of power. Women were seen as the victims of an oppressive patriarchal social order. From a variety of feminist perspectives, several authors examined how the female body was regulated, normalized, fetishized and commodified in a range of consumerist discourses (Dyer 1982; Winship 1983; Kilbourne 1995). Early feminist research on women's magazines of the mid-1970s, for example, drew attention to the fact that consumer representations of the female body – on the cover or in features – routinely normalized women by portraying them as glamorous, sexual, domestic and usually white (Winship 1983). Similarly, other feminist scholars pointed out that in discourses of advertising and fashion, the female body was consistently the reference point for the persuasion to consume (Kilbourne 1995; McRobbie 1996). Fragmented, sexualized and commodified, women's bodies were merely the objects of consumption, the signs of representations, rather than resources to be deployed in practices of self-fashioning.

Some feminists, however, have argued that a narrow focus on the domination and objectification of women in contemporary consumer culture obscures women's active engagement with their bodies. They have suggested that a view of women as the passive accomplices in their own objectification is overly pessimistic. Hence, attempts have been made at a theoretical level to conceptualize agency and the female body and examine the way in which consumer culture may have provided women with important resources to become embodied subjects. From their research on women's and girls' magazines, for example, Winship (1983) and McRobbie (1994b) have shown that consumption practices have become an increasingly important source for the creation of an individualized feminine self. Women are now exhorted to engage in the 'work of femininity' by purchasing mass-produced commodities and transforming these into expressions of their own unique identity. Based on the idea that beauty is not naturally given but achievable by all through the correct application of diverse products, women are encouraged to work on their bodies, labouring to perfect an ever-increasing number of zones. Mouth, hair, legs, eyes, teeth and other bodily parts must all be subject to scrutiny in order to achieve their ideal feminine self (Winship 1983). According to this view, women become active agents of their own self-fashioning. Similarly, Smith (1990) has introduced the idea of women as 'secret agents' behind gendered discourses of femininity. In her view, when women confront consumer discourses that inform them that their body is inferior, a gap is created between the body as deficient and the body as an object to be remedied. Dissatisfaction becomes an energizing process – the motivation for women to engage with their bodies as an object for work, for 'doing femininity'. Feminist critics have argued therefore that the view of women as merely recipients and unquestioning transmitters of cultural meanings of femininity is too limited. They have suggested that, rather than simply adopting versions of femininity that they are invited to emulate, women actively seek to redefine and rearticulate the meaning of these femininities (Lury 1996; McRobbie 1996). They may resist or subvert normative discourses of femininity and exploit them in new ways. They are active subjects who can take pleasure in specifically female modes of consuming. For instance, Cixous (1994), taking difference as a starting point for exploring the specific features of feminine embodiment, has pointed to the pleasures of fashion, arguing that it can materialize the most intimate sensations. The fashion garment is not simply an object but a sensibility that constitutes a woman's aesthetic inclinations. Fashion does not merely reshape the body but becomes continuous with it. It is a new way of speaking with the body, liberating it from silence. Fusing identity with appearance, the inside with the outside, fashion can be a form of self-expression. According to Cixous, then, desires and subjectivity can be enunciated through consuming fashion. By providing insights into the materiality of feminine embodiment, Cixous suggests that it is not simply oppressive but that it can be empowering as well.

The concepts of masquerade and narcissism have also been deployed in analyses seeking to identify a distinctively feminine relation to consumer culture. Lury (1996), for instance, has suggested that women have subverted the idea that beauty is something that can be achieved and have developed ways of seeing femininity as a masquerade. In her view, this enables women to play with their personal identity and take pleasure in the adoption of diverse roles and masks. Similarly, Evans and Thornton (1989) have argued that fashion is one of the many costumes of the 'masquerade of femininity' and can enable women to manipulate their social position. As they have pointed out, with every change of style or appearance 'the body can be made through dress, to play the part it desires as gender coding is displaced from the body on to dress' (Evans and Thornton 1989: 62). In their view, costumes can be worn on the street as 'semiotic battledress' (Evans and Thornton 1989: 14).

From this perspective, the process of masquerade or the 'simulation of femininity' has a liberatory potential in the creation (and subversion) of diverse female subjectivities and enables temporary resistances to impositions of power, including the operation of the male gaze. According to Lury (1996), this more active understanding of women's participation in consumption practices can be used to explain the emergence of the ironic and self-conscious manipulation of style that characterizes contemporary consumer culture. A similar point has been made by McRobbie (1996), who suggests that, in a range of commercial discourses and cultural forms, women are constituted as 'knowing' consumers, well able to recognize how they are being persuaded to consume. In her view, the mocking humour, irony, parody and refusal of feminine naïvety in consumer-led discourses provides a space for a degree of reflexivity and critique by women of the normative practices of femininity.

Other writers have made use of the concept of narcissism and re-evaluated it positively as a source of specifically feminine pleasure. Partington (1991), for example, has argued that, historically, for women to invite the male gaze they have had to become skilled in discriminating between objects and using them to adorn themselves and their environment. These skills of looking have become the basis of women's shared knowledges and pleasures. In her view, 'Female subjectivity is acquired through learning-to-look as well as learning-to-be-looked-at' (Partington 1991: 54). Hence, to exercise such skills in judgements or expressions of taste, women have become subjects of a (female) voyeuristic gaze while at the same time identifying narcissistically with commodities because they themselves are constituted as *objects* of the male gaze. In this view, a specific female subjectivity provides the basis for the emergence of an aestheticized mode of using objects and creating one's own identity. Similarly, authors such as Lipovetsky (1994) have discussed the narcissistic pleasures of transforming oneself, 'feeling like – and becoming – someone else, by using cosmetics and changing the way one dresses' (Lipovetsky 1994: 79).

Although the above perspectives identify women as subjects of a gaze, active in the construction and display of a simulated feminine identity, women are still not in a position to refuse the male gaze. As Lury (1996) has pointed out, although women may now adopt a playful, imitative attitude to self-presentation, this cannot be construed as a strategy of resistance in situations where women do not have the power directly to avoid the male gaze. They may simply sidestep its force by using it for their own ends. In her view, it is a compensatory practice, a relation of displacement, in which the subjects and objects of consumer culture are confused. According to Lury (1996), then, cultural resources for the creation of the modern self are not equally available to all. A feminine identity cannot be realized as cultural capital nor legitimated as symbolic capital nor exchanged as economic capital. Women are constrained in the construction of identity because their consumption practices tend to be carried out in relations of power and under material circumstances that limit their ability for self-fashioning (Lury 1996). Similarly, Winship (1983) and McRobbie (1994a) have also suggested that despite the language of 'choice', the 'work of femininity' can be seen as the imposition and enactment of a cultural ideal of feminine beauty. Women are still expected to adhere to the perfect body shape and thereby seek approval of the male gaze. A similar point has been made by Rabine (1994) in relation to fashion when she argues that the fashion-conscious woman is encouraged to become a self-producing subject. By putting on clothes and using cosmetics, she is encouraged to enact the fantasies of fashion magazines on her body. These daily rituals are pleasurable, not only because they are 'erotically charged', but because they make the body seem changeable, thus satisfying desires for control and novelty. The contradiction is that, at the very moment when women are portrayed as self-producing, what they are frequently constructing is the normative and subjugated image of the heterosexually desirable female (Rabine 1994). As Lury (1996) has pointed out, if women continue to subscribe to male-defined cultural ideals of feminine beauty, if they cannot exercise ownership of their own selves, then they cannot easily acquire other forms of cultural capital either.

However, in exploring the tensions in cultural discourses of feminine beauty and fashion, these authors have developed an understanding of consumption practices as both an expression of the objectification of women and an opportunity to become an embodied subject. Indeed, the contradictory nature of consumption for women has been well described by Myers (1986), who sees it as verging on a form of cannibalism. She argues that women are defined as both the consumers of products and as consumers of themselves as commodities, 'as images to be "consumed" by the gaze of men' (Myers 1986: 137). Women are, therefore, simultaneously the consumers and the consumed – the subjects and objects of consumption.

An examination of a particular consumption activity – body building – exemplifies the complexities of women's relationship to consumer culture and the way in which women negotiate their contradictory positioning when attempting to assert their own subjectivity.

Body building and female subjectivity

Practices such as body building make visible questions of identity and embodiment; how contemporary identities are constructed through and in the body. The body builder (male and female) seeks to rewrite the self by rewriting the physical body. She or he seeks to construct and negotiate her or his identity through 'body work' and transformation (Benson 1997). In this section, however, we are concerned specifically with female body builders. For it can be argued that the issue of body building raises questions concerning what is an acceptable female body shape and image. More importantly, it is a bodily practice that illustrates the contingent and insecure conditions under which women attempt to assert their subjectivity through reflexively fashioning their own identities.

To elaborate, body building is a purposive activity whereby women aim to produce a particular bodily form, a body that fulfils certain criteria in terms of muscle size, shape, definition and tone. To this extent, it is an explicit and conscious process of self-transformation. Women body builders speak of their bodies with pleasure. They enjoy feelings of empowerment and the fruits of exerting extreme self-control and mastery of the body (Johnston 1996). This is hardly surprising, for, as Bordo (1993) has pointed out, contemporary cultural discourses valorize control of the body as indicative of one's moral worth. For many women body builders, then, engaging in this activity is a way of asserting their female subjectivity. As one woman expressed,

> The beauty of body building is you can change your appearance. By your own efforts you can add or substract pounds of body weight. You can build your arms, shoulders, legs, chest, back, and in so doing, you can get pleasure from training you might never have dreamed possible.
>
> (From *Female Body Building*, July 1989: 4; quoted in Mansfield and McGinn 1993: 65)

However, although body building suggests the correct management of desire (Bordo 1993) through regimens of self-management, there are problems for women. Women body builders, according to Kuhn (1988), pose a twofold challenge to the natural order. This is because the body functions as an 'irreducible sign of the natural, the given, the unquestionable' (Kuhn 1988: 16) and, simultaneously, as a signifier of sexual difference. In other words, the body is assumed to be the fixed biological determinant of human subjectivity. Other cultural assumptions about what it means to be 'female' and 'male' derive from this a priori 'natural' difference. Thus, when women enter the arena of body building and deliberately sculpt their bodies through purposive activity, not only are notions of the naturalness of the body disrupted but also binary notions of femininity and masculinity – the bodily-centred meanings of sexual difference. As Kuhn (1988) has pointed out, muscles carry a great deal of cultural meaning in relation to the 'naturalness' of sexual difference and, significantly, in contemporary consumer culture muscularity is coded as masculine. Thus, in Kuhn's view, there is a double transgression involved in female body building: 'Not only is the naturalness of the body called into question by its inscription within a certain kind of performance; but when women have muscles, the natural order of gender is under threat as well' (Kuhn 1988: 17). The female body builder is therefore seen as a deviant and dangerous figure who offers a threat both to the feminine and the masculine. When muscularity has the possibility of being equated with femininity and of becoming an expression of female subjectivity, then the relationship between masculinity and muscularity is also called into question.

Anxieties about female strength have provoked controversies in the body building industry. In discussing the diverse ways in which the industry has responded to this perceived threat, Mansfield and McGinn (1993), adopting a Foucauldian framework, have examined a number of interlocking discourses and discursive practices that together provide the conditions under which women body builders attempt to negotiate their self-identities. They have examined the way in which the body building community – by which they mean the judges and the sponsors of contests, the body building magazines and the regulating bodies – attempt to police acceptable femininity and 'make safe' for social, cultural and economic consumption the figure of the woman body builder. For example, an examination of body building magazines suggests that discourses around the use of steroids are sex-specific. Whereas stories about steroid use among male body builders concentrate on the health risks and rarely focus on the emasculating consequences of excessive use, those about women body builders concentrate on their 'loss of femininity'. One article they cite by Ferguson (1990) mentions the problems of an 'enlarged clitoris, increased or decreased libido, decreased breast size, diminished menstruation, increased aggressiveness' (Ferguson 1990: 57; quoted in Mansfield and McGinn (1993: 60)). Thus, for women, it is the threat that the use of steroids poses to their 'feminine' identity that is seen as undesirable. Similarly, Mansfield and McGinn point out that judges of contests operate with a notion of a correct female body. Thus, those women who 'go too far' – beyond the bounds of acceptable femininity by becoming 'too muscular' or 'too vascular' – are unlikely to win contests. The judging of contests is therefore one of the major sites where ambivalences about women and muscularity are rendered visible. But more importantly for contestants, these judges are in a position of power to enforce their notions of acceptable femininity. Women's attempts to assert their subjectivity through body building are contingent on their evaluations and decisions. In terms of the sponsors, Mansfield and McGinn cite an instance in 1990 where Reebok refused to sponsor a women's body building contest on the grounds that they were unhappy with the appearance of several competitors. Such discourses and discursive practices, they argue, shape and constrain women's attempts at self-fashioning, particularly since many women see competitions as an important part of body building (Mansfield and McGinn 1993: 51). If, through bodily practices, they 'stray too far' from acceptable notions of femininity, their identities as 'real' women are rendered insecure.

How, then, do competitors respond? One response to this situation is for competitors to engage in 'compensatory practices'. According to

Mansfield and McGinn (1993), they try to walk the line between muscularity and acceptable femininity by adopting traditional signifiers of femininity in order to counter-balance their musculature. They adopt the blonde 'Barbie doll' look of the hyper-feminine, use lipstick, make-up and nail polish and adopt a posing style that emphasizes their grace and creativity (Mansfield and McGinn 1993). In other words, adopting the caricature features of femininity and elements of parodic excess is one way in which women body builders fashion their bodies to fulfil the constraints of aesthetically safe femininity. These physical practices are 'reiterative and citational practices' (Butler 1993) that evoke and reproduce normative, cultural images of femininity.

While this parodic enactment of femininity reveals the 'masquer-ade' of 'real' femininity, at the same time it exposes the discursive and institutional constraints that impinge on women body builders when constructing their identities. Although contemporary female identities are constructed in and through the body, there is a tension between the capacity for self-fashioning and the constraints of the locations of their enactment. The self-reflexive fashioning of female subjectivity therefore frequently operates within sets of power rela-tions and material and social contexts that constrain women to act in certain ways. Female body builders, however, are a potential source of 'gender trouble' (Butler 1989) precisely because they upset normative conceptions of the appropriate female body. Although body building may confirm and support stereotypical notions of femininity and is not always empowering for those who engage in it, it does create a symbolic space that offers new possibilities for experimenting with alternative identities.

Conclusion

This chapter has examined the extent to which the body plays a mediating role between consumption and self-identity and has become a key site for the marking of difference. It has suggested that consumer culture provides embodied subjects with many of the cultural, symbolic resources for reflexive self-fashioning (Featherstone 1991a; Giddens 1991) which can be used in strategies of distinction (Bourdieu 1984). However, it has been suggested that there is some dispute between authors with regard to the nature of the links be-tween consumption, identity and the body. For Bourdieu we consume according to our social class position; consumption choices become imprinted on the body, establishing social differences. The prescriptive determinism of his concept of habitus, however, does not allow for the possibility that social subjects may adopt a playful and ironic approach to their identities. Although Bourdieu's model is not entirely static, he does not suggest theoretically how people may break free from the corporeal trajectories assigned to them by class location

(Shilling 1993). Whereas for Bourdieu, however, the body remains a real entity, a materialization of class taste, for postmodern theorists such as Jameson (1985) and Baudrillard (1983) the body becomes merely the bearer of the endless reduplication of signs. Although these theorists allow for identities that are fluid and subject to change depending on consumption preferences, bodies defy readability in their formulations. Hence, from a postmodern perspective, it is difficult to see how judgements of taste or status – strategies of distinction – are possible. Although it has been suggested that the overproduction of goods, images and information leads to problems of misreading signs (Featherstone 1991b, 1995), nevertheless social inequalities do persist. Importantly, approaches that focus narrowly on class or that even ignore social differences cannot account for the particularities of women's embodied experiences. Hence, it has been left to feminists to redress this imbalance.

Given that access to cultural resources for reflexive self-fashioning is not equally available to men and women, feminists have pointed to the problematic and often contradictory position that women are in. By exploring women's negotiations of cultural discourses of appropriate femininity they have developed a framework for understanding bodily practices as both an expression of the objectification of women's bodies and an opportunity for them to become embodied subjects (K. Davis 1997b). Analyses deploying concepts of masquerade and narcissism have shown that women have a distinctive relationship to consumer culture – one that is playful, pleasurable, parodic, even potentially empowering. Nevertheless, to the extent that men still have the power to judge how women look, their claims to self-definition, to be self-producing, are frequently on shaky ground (Lury 1996). Hence, until women themselves can be socially recognized as 'cultural intermediaries' and thereby the instigators of cultural change, the possibility of an alternative body politics is limited. Signs that this may be happening, however, can perhaps be seen in the work of artists such as Jenny Savage, Alison Watts and the photographer Cindy Sherman, who are exploring the possibilities of producing not merely transgressive images of women, but wider transformations in bodily aesthetics.

Further reading

A good introduction to work on consumption is Bocock, *Consumption* (1993), which analyses the main postwar features of consumer society, its historical development and various theoretical approaches such as Marxist, poststructuralist, psychoanalytic and postmodern perspectives. A more general collection of work on consumption and identity is Mackay (ed.) (1997) *Consumption and Everyday Life*, which focuses on how individuals appropriate and make sense of various cultural forms in routine, everyday settings. For an empirical study of the relationship between consumption practices and self-identity, see Lunt and Living-stone (1992), *Mass Consumption and Personal Identity: Everyday Economic Experience*. An overview of the centrality of the body in sociological thought is provided by Shilling (1993) *The Body and Social Theory*. In particular, he provides an excellent and detailed review of Bourdieu's work on the body, class and identity. Given the centrality of feminism to debates about the body, identity and consumption, several texts can be noted as being useful. These include K. Davis (ed.) (1997a), *Embodied Practices*, which contains various articles examining the role of the body as socially shaped territory and as the site of individual women's struggles for autonomy and self-determination; Wilson and Ash (1992), *Chic Thrills*, which examines links between fashionable bodies and modern identities from a postmodern perspective; Bordo (1993), *Unbearable Weight: Feminism, Western Culture, and the Body*, which explores how domination is enacted on and through female bodies in consumer culture; and, for an alternative view, Radner (1995), *Shopping Around: Feminine Culture and the Pursuit of Pleasure*, which draws on Freud's concepts of narcissism to explore specifically female pleasures in consumption. For further reading on body building, which includes an empirical study of participants' perceptions, see Johnston (1996), 'Flexing femininity: female body-builders refiguring "the body" ' in *Gender, Place and Culture*. Since negotiations of racial and ethnic identities in consumer culture remain unexplored in this chapter, a useful text for further consultation is Gilroy (1993), *The Black Atlantic: Modernity and Double Consciousness*.

CHAPTER **4**

Old bodies

EMMANUELLE TULLE-WINTON

Then he said a beautiful thing: 'You are living in symbiosis
with the disease. Go away and continue to do so.'
(Rose 1997: 93)

Introduction

Old bodies are problematic: they can cause us pain, devalue our social
and cultural status and in the end they remind us of our finality.
Gillian Rose was still in her middle years when she was diagnosed
with cancer. The above quotation finds her in what we often refer to
as the terminal stages of cancer: after several operations and sessions
of radiation the disease seemed to have conquered her body, and this
process could no longer be controlled by the best invasive medical
technology. But for a while her body and her disease reached a level
of equilibrium which allowed her to begin to think about accom-
modating to her cancer rather than fruitlessly expending energy fighting
it. Somehow – as was pointed out to her by her surgeon – she was
living in symbiosis with her disease. She seemed to have reached a
level of intimacy with her bodily processes and thus could start re-
sponding to her illness on a more rational level. I wonder whether the
opportunity to relate to our bodies in a similar way is open to us as we
become old.

In this chapter I propose to examine the ways in which old age has
been embodied in the modern period – that is, since the emergence in
the late eighteenth century of the modern understanding of old age.

Embodiment refers to the ways in which bodily or corporeal processes are intertwined with and moulded by social processes (Woodward 1997). The argument I will follow is that old age has been understood primarily in relation to its corporeality – its bodily manifestations – in a framework that has given primacy to the biomedical dimension of corporeality and, in the process, excluded the social dimension of being old. This, it will be argued, has given rise to constructions of old age that have facilitated and also justified the relegation of old people and their bodies to the margins of social life and also, interestingly, of sociology. In other words, old people and their bodies have been perceived as different, as other, and their otherness, in its various manifestations, has in its turn constituted them as old.

These processes of interpretation and attendant practices of segregation have been detrimental to old people. In contemporary society, ageing is a process that we have been inclined to fear and the negative aspects of being old are often held up as justification for these fears. There is no doubt that old age is often accompanied by disability or pain and that it is a reminder of human finitude (Biggs 1999), especially in its later stages; and our relationship to our ageing process is often one of conflict and helplessness. There is nevertheless an argument for seeking alternative ways of imagining old age, both theoretically and experientially, in order to live in symbiosis rather than in conflict with our ageing bodies.

Attempts have been made in social gerontology (the study of the social aspects of ageing and old age) to offer alternative theoretical accounts of old age. Interestingly, these have either taken the biological body for granted or elided it entirely from the ageing experience, instead foregrounding the social and the cultural, leading to Öberg's (1996) remark that the body is absent from social gerontology. Although it seems to be a positive move towards a more socially sensitive way of locating old age, it is nevertheless problematic. This foregrounding has been effected through an extension of middle age and the regulation of the body aimed at the elision of the visible signs of old age. This chapter will conclude that it is this corporeal dimension, in its interaction with the sociostructural context in which we become old, that has to be recovered. This may perhaps lead us to imaginings of old bodies that are not necessarily predicated on their disappearance.

The chapter will be structured as follows: first, to set the scene, I will examine, in general terms, the failure of sociology and of social gerontology to challenge received ideas about old bodies and the way they affect the experience of old age. To this end I will highlight the marginalization of old age in sociology, the role played by sociology in the dissemination of the dominant discourse of old age and the restricted forms of embodiment that are a characteristic of this discourse. This will allow me to argue that the sociological imagination can help us to ask more productive questions about old age and old bodies. The focus here, inspired by traditional social theory, will be on linking modernist conceptions of old age with the production of unwanted bodies. Second, as an illustration of these processes of marginalization, I will examine the ways in which old age and its bodies are represented. The restricted and restrictive nature of these representations, and their association with a set of narratives that foreground loss of attractiveness and malfunction, will give rise to a set of reflections, in the third section, on the formation of the dominant discourse of old age, as it relates to its embodiment. As a starting point, I shall use the emergence of the senile body and explore its resonance in the regulation of old people. Here the medicalization of old age, the professionalization of the problems of old age and the theorizing of old age around concepts of disengagement and individual adaptation to loss will be described. Subsequent theoretical developments have offered the prospect of rearticulating old age by focusing away from the body and looking at the structural and cultural determinants of old age. I will examine the extent to which these rearticulations represent a form of resistance to more orthodox approaches and particularly liberation from the tyranny of the body in decline. It is in the last two sections that I will examine alternative ways of imagining old age and its embodiment, particularly its reconceptualization into a polymorphous body that is at once socially located and emotionally vibrant. But first I will outline the theoretical backbone for the analysis to follow.

Theorizing old bodies

The focus of this chapter appears to justify drawing on the work of Michel Foucault, particularly *Discipline and Punish* (1977), the three volumes of *The History of Sexuality* (1978, 1985 and 1986) and his other writings on government and regulation (Foucault 1979). In this work the body was given prominence because, he argued, it is inscribed with the manner of its regulation. It is like a text from which can be read the social, economic and cultural forms of life that are contemporaneous to it (Prado 1995). Foucault's approach is intimately linked with his distinctive understanding of power and resistance to power, as outlined below.

I will adopt a genealogical approach to delineate the constitution of the dominant discourse of old age and of its corporeality as it emerged in the late eighteenth century and developed to the present. Foucault was critical of traditional historical understandings of social change, particularly as they were premised on the existence of a grand design in the progression of man and civilization towards perfection and greater and more accurate knowledge. According to Foucault, historical discourse explicitly relied on a conception of social change as a linear, continuous progression from an imperfect beginning through a better present all the way to a perfect future (Prado 1995). Foucault rejected this premise and instead advocated an approach that focused on the emergence, the 'coming-to-be' (Prado 1995: 36), of systems of interpretations or discourses connecting events and their role in making particular types of social action possible. This approach is pertinent here and will underpin the structure of the argument developed in this chapter. This is because the modern discourse of old age has slowly gained in density through a series of shifts rather than evolving in a neat linear way. These shifts did not necessarily succeed one another but in many cases emerged in response to others without entirely displacing them, thus spawning a range of parallel ideas of what it is possible to accomplish and expect in old age linked by a common thread. It is the 'coming-to-be' of this complex discursive network that I will chart throughout this chapter.

I will show that Foucauldian theoretical handles (discourse, regulation and resistance) can take us so far but that they do not allow us to deal with the lived experience of being old. A focus on the gendered nature and the lived experience of growing old will point us in the direction of phenomenology as a space for imagining ways of being old that take corporeality on board.

Old bodies and the sociological imagination

The past 15 years or so have seen a surge of interest in the body and this has produced different ways of imagining bodies (K. Davis 1997a). The extent to which old age has benefited from this trend is worthy of interest.

This is a pertinent concern given the distinct lack of interest shown by sociology in old age and in what it is like to become and be old (Phillipson 1998). Turner (1996: 246) argues that sociology's recent neglect of old age reflected the lack of a sociology of the body – that is, the inability to integrate 'research on the biological dimensions of life with the social and cultural features'. It also reflected popular stereotypes about old people, usually centred around the inevitability of old age and its manifestation as physical decrepitude from which cultural irrelevance could be inferred. Old age was therefore outside the social because it was an essentially biological process. And yet old age, and age generally, encompasses at least three interrelated dimensions – chronological, physiological and social (Arber and Ginn 1995). Of these three dimensions the last two are particularly relevant: physiological age, itself a construct that has its roots in the reappropriation of corporeality and the ageing process by biomedicine, and social age. Social age refers to the set of social and cultural practices that punctuate the life course, such as institutional age (the age at which one can vote or retire for instance), and also the types of expectations that frame our life choices and that, although not necessarily inscribed in law, nevertheless guide us on what is permissible for us to accomplish at particular points in time. Bury (1995) adds that most expert commentaries about old age have emanated from (social) gerontology –

the study of old age – and thus have tended to be restricted to policy and management rather than shedding light on the processes leading to the production of what is called old age. In other words, sociological neglect reflects two interrelated and self-referential processes: first, the conflation of the bodies of old people with the lived experience of being old and, second, the construction of the corporeality of old age as no more than a biological process in its terminal stages.

Thus, traditionally, sociology has failed to locate old age at the intersection of 'the personal troubles of milieu and the public issues of social structure' (Mills 1967: 8). In this way it has played a role in the production and reproduction of the dominant discourse on old age, rather than revealing the practices, structures of thought and habits of speech that constituted the discursive framework on which we came to know old age. However, more recently, sociological inquiry has been useful in reflecting on the normative role of sociological theorizing, particularly in the field of ageing and old age, enabling us to ask different questions about being old that reflect the diversity of human experience, not just cross-culturally but also in identifiable cultural entities. A sociological approach will therefore be used to ask how we come to know ourselves in old age and how, in particular, we relate to our bodies as they age.

Old bodies are ubiquitous in western societies at the beginning of the twenty-first century. Some people view this phenomenon with alarm. I will not here rehearse the arguments about the legitimacy of what Katz (1992: 204) referred to as 'alarmist demography' – that is, the problematizing of population ageing as an actuarial problem, rather than greeting it as a miracle of longevity to which more and more can aspire. Yet, as Öberg (1996) has argued, sociology and social gerontology have paid little attention to the corporeality of becoming and being old. He bemoans the absence of a *phenomenological* dimension of the body in past and recent accounts of the ageing experience, including the foundational works produced by the grandees of US gerontology (for instance, Birren and Bengtson 1988 – see Further reading).

Öberg further asserts that the bodies of old people, although not really missing from the discourse of old age, are made known to us only in a specific framework of interpretation, from which experience is inferred: the medicalized body and the malfunctioning body. To this I would add the body hidden from view, confined in specialist housing. This is not just the absent-presence of corporeality that Shilling (1993) signals – where the fleshiness of the body is not deemed an important aspect of the social – but its restriction to a single dimension, one that lacks fleshiness or emotional content. Although at the level of individual experience the loss of function in parts or the whole of one's body may be catastrophic, to quote Sacks (1985: xiv), 'nature's richness is to be studied . . . in the endless forms of individual adaptation by which human organisms, people, adapt and reconstruct themselves, faced with the challenges and vicissitudes of life'. Elsewhere Cole (1997) laments the restricted ways in which old age has been constructed in professional and expert discourse, focusing primarily on loss of function and its management or on 'attitudes' towards elderly people, leaving untouched the spiritual and existential dimensions that those journeying through old age may want to reclaim.

Representing old bodies

This restriction is nowhere more evident than in the ways in which old people and their bodies are represented in the contemporary period, especially in the visual arts such as photography. Featherstone and Hepworth (1989), Featherstone and Wernick (1995) and Blaikie and Hepworth (1997) have highlighted the salience of this 'cultural iconography': visual representations of old people provide us with images of what it is to be old. These images serve as models against which we can assess whether we are old. They provide us with models of appropriate expectations and conduct, and they also illustrate deep-seated collective and personal fears about the 'reality' thus represented. In his study of representations of the 'stages of life' and of 'characters' such as the old crone in Classical Antiquity and later, Hepworth (1995) highlighted their dual nature: they were idealized representations that may or may not have corresponded to the reality of becoming old in Antiquity and in the Middle Ages – after all, fewer people than in the present could reasonably expect to go through each successive stage – but they alluded to a preferred reality. On the other hand, they conveyed strong moral warnings against undesirable characteristics and these were most effectively *embodied* in old age: a powerful example was the old crone who acted as a symbol of and warning against what a life of sexual excess and vanity would yield.

In Featherstone and Wernick's (1995) edited collection contributors map out the boundaries of the representable and its symbolic meanings in the contemporary period. What comes across forcefully is that contemporary practices of representing old bodies carry a normative, moralizing content as powerful as those of the Ancients or the Victorians. Featherstone and Wernick (1995) and Hepworth (1995) critically explore images of positive ageing – as conveyed by the trendy retirement magazines that started to appear in the late 1970s – and their potential for liberation from the alienation of negative stereotypes of old people and of the old body. Indeed, these images seem to provide old people with a new space in which to maintain identity. They do so by presenting innocuous photographs of usually affluent, *well-preserved* older people who are invited to locate themselves in an extended midlife rather than in old age. The photographic conventions used in these magazines are designed to smooth out the aesthetic deficiencies of old bodies – by choosing attractive models who are usually young-looking, and presenting them in soft focus or, in more recent publications, engaged in sporting activity. These bodies have particular obligations to fulfil: to remain both presentable and financially independent post-retirement. These are in sharp contrast to less favourable and less appealing images – those that stress very old age and dependence. Bytheway and Johnson (1998: 255) note that photographic representations belong to the symbolic order because their aim is recognition – that is, the *correct* interpretation of the picture as representing a typical image of old age. This can be conveyed by using three strategies, one of the most obvious being to 'focus attention upon the body and, in particular, the various signifiers of age'. Johnson and Bytheway (1997) analysed 270 photographs depicting old people in a care situation. In contrast to the affluent subjects on Featherstone and Hepworth's magazine covers, the messages conveyed here were of people dependent on help from professional carers, usually in institutional settings. Their advanced age was made obvious to the onlooker by the carefully controlled depiction of the bodily signs of old age in the context of the institution. But the subjects were shown fully clothed and smiling, eschewing more graphic representations of bodily decrements. This did not detract from the power of these images: the photographs successfully acted as a warning that we too may end up like this.

There are indeed very few graphic representations of old bodies. The few that exist usually shock and attract revulsion. Woodward (1991) describes reactions to a display of photographs at a conference on the body in US culture. One photograph was of an old man, or rather of an old man's body, shown naked, changed by the passage of time and bearing the familiar marks of wear and tear. It was also a body that bore the evidence of the vicissitudes of a past life, a very personal body. The photograph evoked disgust and even outrage among conference participants, including, and especially, in those firmly settled in midlife. It was described as exploitative, disturbing and unjustifiable. I encountered the same response when I showed a few photographs to a group of undergraduates, some of whom were practising nurses working with sick bodies. The photographs, taken by Donigan Cumming (1996), were of a Canadian journalist and latterly actress (Nettie Harris) when she was in her late 70s until her death at the age of 81. The pictures were taken over a period of 10 years in the woman's apartment, with her active consent and participation. They played with a set of conventions of representations of young female bodies: at once replete with sexuality but belonging to the domestic sphere. In this instance these were not ironic transgressions. They conveyed in several layers a complex of moods and feelings not usually associated with the bodies of old women: barely repressed sexuality and voluptuousness but also the rejection of the traditional canons of feminine beauty, the aesthetic quality of old bodies – her own and also those of others sometimes sitting with her for the portraits. The emaciation of her naked body was also frankly represented, usually in the stark surroundings of a white tiled bathroom, juxtaposed with representations of her body half or fully clothed, sometimes carefully to evoke sexuality and at other times dishevelled, surrounded by the disorder of domestic life. There was no evocation here of graceful ageing, of positive ageing, nor, for that matter, any suggestion of dependency on carers. There was no attempt to disguise or cover her agedness, but rather the effect was to convey it in all its complexities, in its familiar surroundings, or in its nakedness. The students declared the photographs almost acceptable because she had a slim body – a good figure for her age, as they put it – thus making them just about worth showing. But most of the time they found the photographs disturbing because they showed the body of an old woman in unconventional and ambiguous ways. They forced the viewer to come face to face with agedness and to imagine another way of being old, outside clinical or care settings. But because these images are not rooted in a recognizable moral framework, they provoke discomfort and are thus rejected. Woodward concludes an assessment of what is representable by saying:

> I submit that the relative lack of ambiguity in our representations of aging, the relative paucity of their elaboration or differentiation, is a symptom that our culture as a whole has not succeeded in producing persuasive representations of aging – in particular of the aging body – which are characterized by *tolerance.* . . .
>
> (Woodward 1991: 8; original emphasis)

Loss and the medicalized body

The reluctance to countenance stark representations of old bodies is consonant with the dominant discourse on old age and I will now delineate this discourse by relying on a range of social gerontologists who have sought their inspiration in Foucault's work.

It is now well established that the body of modernity is first and foremost a medicalized body – that is, a body subjected to the medical gaze (Foucault 1963) (see Chapter 2 for a more complete analysis of this process). Katz (1996) and Cole (1997) argue that the same can be said of the old body and they go on to describe a range of processes through which the bodily afflictions experienced by some old people – and particularly old women – were made legible to modern sensibilities and modern problematizations. They identify the emergence of clinical medicine at the end of the eighteenth century and the early interest of French clinicians such as Charcot (who died in 1893) in the biological attributes of old age. Clinical medicine became the dominant framework within which the old body assumed its modern complexion. The old body was recognized as a distinct and coherent biological entity with shape and volume signifying the passage of time. Throughout the nineteenth century, the clinical map of the old body was drawn and found its institutional expression in the formation of geriatrics, a term coined by Nascher and made public with the publication in 1914 of his book entitled *Geriatrics*. Geriatrics was therefore the branch of medicine dedicated to the study and classification of senile pathology (its emergence as a separate field of medical practice institutionalized in specialist health service provision came much later, in the 1950s). Far from being a minor form of reappropriation of old age, medicalization was the prime modality of its embodiment. Medicine decontextualized the bodies of old people and reinterpreted them as biological organism with its own properties and laws, and with the perceptual markers thus produced, gave rise to the formation of a new discourse on old age. Thus medicine literally produced the *old body* as object of expertise and also as experiential reference.

Katz (1996) identified three dimensions in which the old body was captured when it was reappropriated by medicine. The first related to the old body as a 'system of signification', a voluminous body that offered itself up as the visible manifestation of disease and loss of strength, framed in a specific and specified anatomical grid. The second related to its 'distinctiveness': the old body was characterized by distinct pathological attributes from the younger adult (male) body, namely degenerative diseases. Linguistically, the old body was senile, where senility had come to mean the occurrence of disease in late life. The third dimension was that of the 'relationship with death': the aged body was the precursor to death. Clinical medicine produced a body that was either normal (disease-free) or pathological (diseased) (Canguilhem 1998). This distinction did not apply well to the old body whose normal state was found in its pathological occurrences and attributes, involved in an inexorable and inherent process of decay and deterioration. Furthermore, this process was said to extend to the deterioration of all intellectual and moral faculties. For old people there was no question of Cartesian dualism and of the maintenance, let alone the construction, of a new sense of self outside the body. Bodily decay was causally related to decline in all other faculties and constituted people as old and as other. In other words, the old body was 'subject constituting' (Katz 1996) and provided its own justification for expectations of appropriate behaviour.

The menopause is a good illustration of these processes. Greer (1991) has argued that biomedicine has constructed an essentially natural process as pathological and therefore opened it to medical intervention. Greer's response to this observation is ambiguous. She did not disagree with the medicalization of menopause per se. Rather it was the conflation of the menopause with the loss of femininity and the entry into decay and, by extension, into new forms of social and cultural marginalization that caused injury to women. In other words, the menopause, in its guise as a medical problem, constituted women as old, redundant, worthless and unattractive. She argued that women should reclaim their right to be old and be freed from the obligation to be sexually available. They should therefore refuse to accept biomedicine's solution to the menopause – the extension of their sexual capital, constructed as a liberating opportunity, obtained through pharmacological intervention – which she argued is another illustration of women's condition of alienation, discipline and surveillance. Elsewhere, Featherstone and Hepworth (1985) and Hepworth and Featherstone (1998) have argued that parallel processes of reappropriation have been applied to male bodies through the *discovery* of the male menopause by nineteenth-century clinicians. This work seemed consonant with expressions of a sense of obsolescence increasingly reported by middle-aged men at that time. It was also linked with the legitimation of expectations of appropriate behaviour in later life: the preservation of one's moral character hinging on the obligation to show sexual restraint.

The problem of old age: the malfunctioning body

If the old body signified systemic and systematic decay, loss and obsolescence, then the problem of its management was posed. The constitutive features of clinical or biomedicine overlapped with the demands of new forms of rules, embodied, according to Foucault (1979), in the emergence of regulation or government as the technique of liberal rule par excellence. Government is the design and application of techniques of surveillance applied to populations and the self by a range of external agencies as well as the self in the pursuit of particular aims – in this instance the control of populations. Social problems and social identities are constructed in the process of identifying appropriate objects and subjects of government. This analysis relies on a different conception of power which, for Foucault (1976a), is not the dense and impermeable attribute of a group or charismatic leader but a way of ordering relationships between social actors and social institutions. Power relations are not fixed and unchanging: they are prone to variations and, in some cases, to being challenged. They are also involved in the generation of dominant values and ideas. Social actors in the modern state take part in their own regulation by adopting techniques with which to control their practices and ways of being, in accordance with the very values and ideas that have currency in a particular discursive framework. One of the principal sites of regulation is, as I have already indicated, the bodies of individuals (Foucault 1984). Therefore, as can be seen, power is dispersed throughout the social organization rather than concentrated in a few hands. It is this dispersion that opens up the possibility for resistance. Because we are all involved in our own regulation, we can also transgress and resist this process.

Biomedicine has taken an active part in the regulation or government of old age and of the old body. As a biomedical entity, with its own internal patterns of (mal)function, the old body was by definition associated with loss and was experienced as such. It is instructive to examine the discursive space in which the corporeality of old age as loss has been addressed: the gerontological discourse.

The emergence of gerontological knowledge reflected, justified and constructed the cultural, economic and symbolic obsolescence of old people (Lynott and Lynott 1996). According to Green (1993), gerontology emerged as the dominant discourse of old age at the beginning of the twentieth century, not as a single discipline but as the empirical space in which old age was to be apprehended and studied, that is recognized. Thus, old age gradually became subjected to multidisciplinary problematizations and attendant empirical investigations: medicine, biology, psychology, social administration and sociology all produced knowledge and narratives about old age, all fuelled by the urge to solve the problem of old age. This urge found its expression in welfare narratives and practices. Here welfare can be defined as a set of practical steps designed to manage physical malfunction as a property of 'the elderly' – that is, as a generalized social problem. Following Foucault (1979), this process was consonant with, first, the identification of a problem population (in this case elderly people), second, the formulation of the problems posed by elderly people and, third, the application of techniques of government on this population and on individuals. Here we are clearly dealing with dimensions extraneous to the clinical mapping of the old body: we are dealing with the social dimension of growing and being old. This is what allows Green (1993) to call gerontology a *social* science, despite its reliance on contributions from the natural sciences (biology and medicine). He argues that gerontology produces 'scientifically formed statements of social knowledge about aging that have public policy relevance' (Green 1993: 45). An early example of the symbiotic relationship between science, medicine and public policy is the statistical work of Adolphe Quételet (1796–1874), who confirmed that, based on the laws of probability, the onset of old age for the 'average man' was 60–5 (Katz 1996). Despite doubts as to their validity, these calculations were used in the design of the retirement policies of western industrialized countries. They gave scientific legitimacy to popular discourses about longevity, about the life led as punctuated by ontologically necessary biological markers and to further subdivisions of late life.

Furthermore, there was a strong semantic relationship between the clinical recognition of senescence in the old body and the social practice of constructing the problem of old age – that is, making old age recognizable as a social and cultural phenomenon. There currently is consensus among a growing number of critical gerontologists (Green 1993; Katz 1996; Phillipson 1998) that the creation of retirement and public pension schemes – alongside other welfare practices – actively contributed to this process, but also to the legitimization of public policy to manage old people. And although concern for the financial and care situation of this population group formed the basis of social policy, other issues such as the apparent cultural marginalization of old people and their propensity to combine retirement with the cessation of activities also became the legitimate focus of expert scrutiny. In gerontological discourse: the old body is invariably inactive, lonely, either at home or in residential care, a victim of its biological decrements.

The disappearance of the old body

I will now focus on theoretical activity in social gerontology, from the point of view of its relationship with the old body. Early theoretical activity (from the 1940s until the late 1970s and early 1980s) reflected the restriction of old age to its physiological and physical dimensions. Lynott and Lynott (1996) reviewed this work and noted that, far from challenging dominant constructions of old age, in fact it contributed to the production of the dominant discourse of old age, presented as the *facts* of old age. In this way, as early as the 1940s the theoretical problem of old age mirrored the experience of being old and was posed in terms of disengagement from the mainstream of society, productive and cultural obsolescence, dependency (that is, dependence on professionals and relatives) and in many cases confinement to institutions.

Turner (1996: 246) describes this theoretical activity as 'in fact merely versions of the functionalist theory of social stratification' as developed by Talcott Parsons. There have, however, been challenges to this particular way of posing the problem of old age. Lynott and Lynott (1996) identified a series of shifts from functionalist approaches, leading to more fundamental redefinitions of the problem of old age as the product of social and cultural processes. Here the bodily manifestations of old age were disregarded and instead the focus shifted to the structural determinants of old age. Thus, on the one hand, old age was produced by public accounts of the facts of ageing (disengagement from paid work, dependence on welfare and the erosion of social and cultural status) and on the other hand, the reality of being old reflected 'the political economy of growing older' (Lynott and Lynott 1996: 754). In the latter view, the facts of old age were no longer seen as inherent features of growing old but were created by the structural features of the wider society, in the service of wealth maximization and the reproduction of the capitalist economy. Estes (1979), Walker (1981) and Phillipson (1982) also argued that a by-product of the marginalization of unproductive elders has been the development of large professional groups in health and social care, servicing the needs of the clients in their care. It was in the interest of welfare providers and other groups living off the problems of old age to nurture dependency and helplessness in old people in order to consolidate their own employment prospects. In this theoretical tradition the blame for the problems of old age was shifted from the individual and his or her physical characteristics to the structural features of capitalism, and the solutions were to be found in fundamental structural transformations, rather than in piecemeal, patchwork programmes of population management.

The scene was therefore set for constructions of old age that did not foreground the body. This shift was encapsulated in de Beauvoir's (1970) statement that being old is not the same as feeling old and, furthermore, that it is a time of ontological insecurity. In this way she anticipated a shift in the discourse on old age based on the separation of the old body from the social, cultural and intimate self.

Governing the declining body

In what follows I will first describe this shift and then evaluate its potential for resisting negative constructions of old age based on declining bodies.

There is a growing body of sociological accounts which in their treatment of old age reflect increasing interest in the ways in which the physical manifestations of growing old are constructed and managed by social actors and what impact they have on self-identity. What this work brings to the surface is the construction of the bodily markers of old age as deterioration and decline, a process that poses a threat to identity and overall integrity because it is a reflection on one's suitability for continued social and cultural belonging.

This has fostered a type of narrative of old age focused on the theme of ageless or unchanging self as a way of effacing bodily deterioration. The old body becomes invisible. In both popular and theoretical narratives the old body is allowed to re-emerge from this position of invisibility only when it begins to hurt and thus becomes a sick body, compromising the integrity of the self by confronting it with its agedness. This takes place in a cultural climate that gives primacy to beautiful and consuming bodies (Shilling 1993) and in which old bodies, with their propensity to undergo changes that transgress dominant aesthetic criteria, are marginalized.

One strategy used by old people to make sense of these visible bodily changes and physical impairments is to conceive of senescence as a mask that covers the real self that lies beneath. This particular strategy – the mask of ageing approach – was explored by Featherstone and Hepworth (1991). It captured the fear of physical deterioration and allowed social actors a way out in a bid to preserve their sense of self. The Cartesian dualism here was exploited and primacy given to the mind, confirmed as the seat of the self. The bodily signs of old age were reinterpreted as the mask which conveyed senescence and obsolescence and beneath which the true person, the real self, lay untouched, unchanged, unadulterated and timeless. This was neatly illustrated in Thompson's (1992) research, which showed that, unless they were physically unwell, his respondents reported that they did not feel old in themselves.

It is also a nostalgic body (Turner 1996) that reflects the passage of time: here old age is experienced as regret for the loss of past physical vigour and aesthetic capital. Cunningham-Burley and Backett-Milburn (1998) noted a similar theme in the ways in which the body was allowed to manifest itself in midlife – that is, at the transition point between maturity and old age – by their middle-aged respondents. Interestingly enough, their findings stemmed from a methodological issue. Having noted that asking informants directly about the impact of the passage of time on their bodies elicited bewilderment, embarrassment and silences, they found that the most acceptable frame in which the respondents would account for these bodily processes was a health-related one (although some of them still found it difficult to relate bodily sensations through language). In this way the authors were able to elicit a range of narratives of the intimate sensations accompanying ageing, one of which pertained to feelings of tiredness and the gradually increasing regulation of physical activity.

The theme of bodily control was also addressed by Vertinsky (1998) in her exploration of the uses of their bodies by women going through the menopause. She found that women's relationship to their bodies was mediated not just by medical intervention but also by stereotypical beliefs about vigorous, strenuous physical activity for women: in the post-reproductive phase – that is, in old age – it is believed to exacerbate the wearing down of bodies. She noted that female athletes, especially older ones, have long been marginalized from, rather than brought into, the mainstream of competitive sport. In later life, this process of marginalization is embodied in the near invisibility of women in sporting events, whether competitive or not. In other words, the paucity of female participation in sports was the outcome of the regulation of female bodies, which in later life is reflected in the urge to *slow down*.

Another strategy is to change the mask, to conceal old age, in what Woodward (1991) calls a game, a masquerade. What she is alluding to is the surgical correction of bodily parts but also, less invasively and more mundanely, the active concealment of the signs of old age through the careful choice of clothing, make-up, the control of one's bearing and so on. Whether it is the encouragement to act one's age (Laz 1998), to age gracefully (Fairhurst 1998) or to will the disappearance of one's agedness and give primacy to a *disembodied* self, what is clearly at stake here is the economy or government of bodies ostensibly to maintain integrity as the key to continued social and cultural relevance. The onus is therefore on individuals to manage their own bodies, inside as well as outside. What this amounts to is the control of the self through particular techniques practised by individuals on themselves (Foucault 1994). The payback for this self-work is the maintenance of cultural relevance, made possible by the extension of middle age (Hazan and Raz 1997) or, in fact, the postponement of old age and its relegation to very old age. This, Hazan and Raz (1997: 269) argue, 'reveals the social efforts to broaden the chronological as well as cultural gap between midlife and old age'. Rather than rehabilitate old age, the disembodiment of the self in later life reinforces the confinement of old bodies to the margins of society. Bodies that cannot be self-regulated because they are too old and uncontrollable become the responsibility of other agencies of government, such as welfare agencies and families, and their otherness is realized through the scientific measurement of their dependency and loss of function.

In the past decade or so in the sociology of old age, there has emerged the lively practice of novelists and other public figures digging out fictional and scholarly accounts of encounters with their old age. These accounts and their analysis in the scholarly literature are designed to enlighten us on the ways in which people cope with growing old, and they usually follow a set formula: the narrator is made aware of the passage of time in a memorable encounter with his or her agedness and its bodily manifestations and then embarks on a nostalgic reflection about the passage of time, the loss of physical attractiveness and their effects on identity. De Beauvoir (1970) describes how a life-threatening illness or physical fatigue brought Walt Whitman, Goethe, Tolstoy and Renoir face to face with their old age. All four devised energy-consuming strategies to override their decrements, involving working at a high level of output to keep decrepitude from consuming them entirely. Bernard Berenson (Bytheway 1993) and J.B. Priestley (Featherstone and Hepworth 1989) were confronted with their agedness when they least expected it, an encounter that gave rise to surprise, an initial lack of recognition and shock. Marcel Proust's *Time Regained* is also an oft-quoted account of a dramatic encounter with old age. Proust describes an encounter with Gilberte, a woman who was the object of his love when both were children, who suggests meeting for dinner. He accepts gladly, but with trepidation adds 'if you don't find it compromising to dine alone with a young man' (Proust 1996: 301) – despite having previously commented on the unflattering marks left on her body and appearance by the passage of time. At this, other guests who had been eavesdropping on the conversation started to laugh and this led him to correct himself and substitute old for young.

Four observations can be made here about the way in which old age is being recognized by these eminent and articulate protagonists. First, it is made evident in its bodily manifestations. Although one may notice it in others, one will also make a spectacle of one's agedness, as others may detect signs of agedness undetected by ourselves. Second, one's encounter with these bodily signs is described as sudden, unexpected and, in the words of Proust (1996: 302), 'a cruel discovery'. Third, the narrator has to readjust his sense of self, which, he claims, is usually fixed in young adulthood, to take account of his changed appearance or the deterioration in his physical health. Fourth, although most old people are women (Arber and Ginn 1995), these well-publicized displays of anxiety in the face of bodily degradation are usually those of men.

Notwithstanding the lack of a well-articulated gender dimension, what is reflected in the above is the problematic nature of the old body for self-recognition. Harper (1997) captures this process by conceiving of the old body as both lived and social. The lived body refers to the experience of interiority, of the intimate sensations conveyed by the body. The social body refers to external appearance, in this case the visibility of agedness. The process of self-recognition in later life can therefore be understood as the tension between the experience of interiority and exteriority – that is, of the ways in which people negotiate the different signals that their lived body and their social body emit to themselves and the outside world. Conceptualizing the old body in this way enables us – social actors and sociologists – to unpack the complex processes implicated in the construction of self in later life and of which corporeality is a constituent element. Thus, bodily sensations and the signals the old body gives off to others are interpreted by social actors in a shared discursive grid, in this case one that devalues the outward signs of agedness.

What also keeps recurring in the above accounts is that one way out of old age is to manage away outward signs of agedness. It is questionable, however, whether this approach amounts to resistance – that is, the construction of strategies that fundamentally challenge the existing discourse and lead to shifts in the distribution of power (Ramazanoglu 1993), in this case in favour of old bodies. To evaluate the success of current approaches to old age in mounting a challenge to the devaluation of old bodies, we have to leave Foucauldian analysis. In the next section I will explore the usefulness of phenomenology to begin charting strategies for the rehabilitation of old bodies and consequently of old age.

Towards a phenomenology of old bodies

Arguing for a phenomenological approach to old age – that is, one that gives embodiment an important place in any understanding of what it is like to be old – impels us to revisit traditional and more recent accounts of the experience of later life. Put together, the accounts delineated earlier in the chapter (the medicalized body, the disabled body, the disengaged body and Öberg's absent body) are as many forms of embodiment: they reflect back to us socially acceptable ways of experiencing the body and of accounting for experience (Gubrium and Wallace 1990). The assault on the self that an encounter with agedness is seen to represent is one dimension of experience. Social actors may, in the next breath, reclaim and reappropriate their agedness (Tulle-Winton and Mooney 1998), especially when asked to justify particular social acts, such as moving to sheltered housing.

As Weiss (1998: 239) argues, we are 'multiple and inconsistent embodied selves'. Thus it is perhaps more appropriate to talk about old bodies, to reflect not only the multiplicity and contiguity of bodily experiences but also, at a structural level, the social and cultural contexts on which social action is contingent. Weiss (1998: 253) also talks about the 'endless chains of possible narratives of embodiment' that can exist simultaneously. She carried out empirical work with (young) Israeli undergraduate students to explore their sense of embodiment. She found that they tended to have recourse to three distinctive but simultaneously occurring narratives of the body: the biological body, the emotive body and the body seen from within. The emotive body referred to inner feelings and compulsion, and the body seen from within referred to the sense of self in the cosmos, as well as the sense of the inner self in the body. The latter was uncontoured, undifferentiated and, puzzlingly enough, ungendered, but would be given shape in response to outside stimuli. The link with the contingencies of everyday experience was played out in the context of the Gulf War and the Iraqi bombings aimed at Israeli targets on Israeli territory. The students had experienced these events as both observers and, in more intimate ways, as bodies under threat and literally given shape by the regulations imposed on Israeli citizens: the wearing of gas masks, confinement to a safe room in the home, listening to radio broadcasts, curfews and so on. These gave rise to narratives of claustrophobia and restraint, inscribed in bodily experience. These intimate feelings lasted beyond the events which gave rise to them.

In the following fictional description of an 87-year-old woman we can see how giving some attention to bodily sensations can yield a more imaginative understanding of late life:

> Her body had, in fact, become her companion, a constant resource and preoccupation, all the small squalors of the body, known only to oneself . . . in old age became dominant and entered into fulfilment of the tyranny they had always threatened. Yet it was . . . an agreeable and interesting tyranny.
>
> (Sackville-West 1983 [1931]: 194)

This account of the relationship between the woman and her old body contrasts with the accounts alluded to previously. Here the body and the changes it undergoes are assumed to be intimately known to the protagonist. What is also conveyed is a sense that this woman's understanding of her body was informed by a lifelong corporeal awareness, rather than one developed suddenly in late life. So her body is not a stranger but something with which she has been in a dialogue for many years.

Csordas (1993: 136) suggests that a phenomenology of the body would recognize 'embodiment as the existential condition in which culture and self are grounded'. Extending this to later life means reclaiming the experience of old age as the interaction between self-generated narratives of bodily sensations and bodily management and the socially, culturally and historically contingent. It also means recognizing the potentially wide variation in sensate experience, between social participants but also within individuals: being old is something we sometimes feel and at other times forget. This shift in and out of feeling old should be accounted for in the way in which we know old age.

Thus the biology is open-ended (Hepworth and Featherstone 1998: 288): it is open to a wide range of meanings and interpretations that are culturally embedded. The case of the menopause is instructive in this respect: it is a 'body-centred' experience and yet its identification as a distinct set of symptoms and signs and the attribution of cause internally in the body is a wholly cultural process, as are the ambiguous meanings attributed to these bodily processes. Here Hepworth and Featherstone (1998), borrow from Merleau-Ponty (1945), who argues that bodily phenomena mediate our relationship to the world around us and are therefore an intrinsic part of ourselves rather than wholly separate. The body is socially and spatially located and is therefore the condition of our engagement with the social. Our carnal experiences therefore cannot exist in themselves, they have to be interpreted and in the mere process of identifying them as significant or otherwise we operate a social act. Therefore corporeality is at once felt and constructed.

Resistant bodies

Old age forces social actors to engage with intimate sensations and their implications for the maintenance of self-integrity or the construction of alternative ways of being in the world. The corporeal is at once constraint and malleable. One can choose to govern the body and keep old age at bay or one can choose to resist government and come to terms with what Williams (1998: 438) called the recalcitrant body. Here he proposes that, regardless of age, the body is ontologically transgressive, uncontrolled and even, in echo of Mellor and Shilling (1997), resistant to rational control. The gerontological discourse has itself generated narratives of the old body in decay which must be managed and even disappeared. But the disappearance of the body using techniques of control, such as surgery, the pressure to age gracefully or the spatial confinement to 'age-appropriate' housing, has limited payback (Tulle-Winton 1999). Far from liberating old people from what Gullette (1997) called the 'narrative of decline', these strategies reinforce the undesirability of being old and merely delay the point at which one will have to face physical deterioration (Biggs 1997; Öberg and Tornstam 1999). Hazan (1986) observed old people in a day centre and the strategies in which they engaged to maintain self-control. Rather than posing a challenge to dominant constructions of old age and disability with a claim to cultural visibility in the mainstream of society, many of the strategies they adopted operated an alternative mechanism of cultural segregation, albeit in terms defined by the members themselves. Any overt display of senility was shunned and members were divided into those who were physically fit enough to walk up to the first-floor room and those who were no longer able to negotiate the stairs. The latter had to stay downstairs, until such time that they would exit the centre, either by dying or by moving to residential care.

The task of critical gerontology and sociology therefore ought to be to imagine ways of being old that defy dominant narratives of old age and look for spaces of resistance where they are least expected. Katz (1997) proposes that we see the loss of bodily function in terms of resistance. Kontas (1998) suggests that we resist the meanings ascribed by others to bodily deterioration by reclaiming control of the conduct of one's life from 'competent' younger people. In cultural terms, this may involve transgressing aesthetic boundaries and accepting, rather than shunning or marginalizing, the biological signs of old age. To date very little research has been done in this area, and especially the gendered nature of the experience of the old body.

Conclusion

To conclude I want to return to Sacks' (1985) quote about the adaptation of the human organism to sickness. If the body is at once flesh and capital, old age is reduced bodily capital. In the dominant discourse of old age, this process of attrition is held up as negative and most narratives of old age have dealt with how social actors *cope* with it. Until the last 20 years the opportunities for engaging with embodiment outside restrictive medical and functional dimensions have been lacking. More recently, space has been made in sociology to view old age as a socially constructed process, and particularly as a process chained to its biological manifestations. This has led to a rejection of the corporeality of old age, arguing that it was extraneous to the social and cultural experience which itself should be given primacy in any understanding of the experience of being old. Keeping at bay the physical discomfort associated with illness and very old age through the adoption of specific techniques of the self and divorcing the self from the body were strategies to resist stereotypical constructions of old people as dependent, incompetent and obsolete bodies in decline. And yet, this has neither led to the tolerance of bodily deterioration nor to the fashioning of forms of embodiment that transgress normative ideas of the body. From a methodological standpoint, we still have few ways of accessing accounts of the emotional effervescence and fleshy consistency of the old body. By putting forward the claim for a phenomenological approach to the old body, I am not simply suggesting that we make room in our understanding of old age for descriptions of bodily processes. Rather, we should develop ways of articulating the intimate ways in which we engage with bodily change, as an individual and also as a cultural strategy.

Further reading

As a general introduction to the linkages between modernity and the production of bodies Marx's *Capital, Vol. 1* (1990) and Wolff's *The Sociology of George Simmel* (1964) will provide a good starting point. To explore these processes further, especially as they relate to the exercise of power and the fashioning of subjects of regulation in the liberal state, Foucault's *Histoire de la sexualité*, translated by R. Hurley as (1978) *The History of Sexuality, Vol. I: An Introduction*, (1985) *The History of Sexuality, Vol. II: The Use of Pleasure* and (1986) *Vol. III: The Care of the Self* as well as (1977) *Discipline and Punish: The Birth of the Prison*, all available in Penguin, should be consulted. J.E. Birren and V.L. Bengtson (1988) *Emergent Theories of Aging* is a good introduction to theorizing on ageing in the social sciences. It provides ample evidence that old age and ageing are indeed prime candidates for theorizing outside biology, but nevertheless disregards the corporeality of old age as a focus worthy of analysis. For a thorough and readable account of the dominant discourse on old age, Katz's (1996) *Disciplining Old Age* is an essential text. Any writings involving Mike Featherstone and Mike Hepworth must be consulted. In relation to the cultural meanings of representation, Featherstone and Wernick's *Images of Aging: Cultural Representations of Later Life* (1995) is an essential starting point. For an immediate confrontation with visible ageing, Donigan Cumming's photographs of Nettie Harris will be found in *Pretty Ribbons* (1996). There is little as yet which deals with the phenomenological dimension of ageing and old age. For an emergent feminist perspective, Kathleen Woodward's *Figuring Age: Women, Bodies, Generations*, published in 1999 by Indiana University Press, brings together contributions that attempt to grasp the corporeality of old women. Greer's *The Change* (1991) is a scathing account of the regulation of old women which attempts to recover old age and experience as an opportunity for symbiosis rather than rejection.

CHAPTER 5

Working bodies

PHILIP HANCOCK AND MELISSA TYLER

Introduction

It could be argued that, at a basic level, the body is simply the medium through which work is carried out. In other words, it is the site of labour power, of the skill and effort deployed in the performance of work. More than this though, the working body is frequently the object of relations of power and control that mould and direct its working activities. It is disciplined, punished or rewarded, depending on its ability to meet the demands placed upon it by the rigours of work. Until relatively recently, however, sociological studies of work and its organization tended to marginalize the significance of the body in analyses of relations of power and control in the workplace. Yet, despite its apparent absence from much of the sociological discourse on work, the body has always been, it could be suggested, implicitly present in one form or another. Today, in response to a number of broad developments – such as shifting philosophical perspectives on the body, changes in working patterns and an increased managerial concern with organizational culture – sociologists have begun to ask questions, more specifically, about the relationship between work, its organization and the human body. This is not to suggest, however, that the body is a 'new' discovery of sociology. With the emergence of the factory system and the rise to dominance of industrial capitalism during the nineteenth century, new problems arose for those concerned with the organization of labour, problems that, as we shall see, were frequently addressed through the bodies of the workforce. What is perhaps most significant today is the academic recognition that the study of the body 'at work' has started to enjoy, which brings with it new opportunities and new challenges.

This chapter opens with a brief discussion of those developments that have provided the impetus for the 'rediscovery and reconsideration' of the working body in sociology and its related disciplines. It then goes on to consider the management and rationalization of the working body under the conditions of capitalist wage labour. Commencing with the development, during the early years of the twentieth century, of managerial systems concerned with the efficient utilization of the bodily capacity for labour, this section charts the refinement of various technologies of rationalization and their eventual impact on the body as a 'material signifier' of organizational life. This conception of the body as a material signifier refers to the idea that the body, as a physical substance, functions as a symbol of a particular organization in much the same way as a company logo or a corporate slogan might. This leads us to an examination of the significant input that feminist-inspired sociology has had for our understanding of the role played by the body in the management of gender differences in the workplace. Finally, we shift our attention away from the domain of wage labour and the work organization to focus on what Shilling (1993) has termed 'body work'. This refers to the time, effort and resources dedicated to maintaining a particular state of embodiment in everyday life. Drawing on the work of Shilling (1993) and Bourdieu (1984) we suggest that this idea potentially offers a way of reconceptualizing the relationship between the act of work and the human body.

Sociology, work and the body

As we noted in the introduction to this chapter, a number of developments in sociology and the world of work have led to a renewed interest in the relationship between the body and the ways in which work is organized according to the conditions of industrial capitalism. First and foremost has been the increasing impact on sociology of a range of critical perspectives on the philosophical tradition bequeathed by the European Enlightenment. Such perspectives – including postmodernism, poststructuralism, feminist theory and critical social theory – have challenged the idea that the mind exists in sovereign relationship to the body and, as such, have legitimated a number of sociological attempts to understand the relationship between society and the body.

It is not, however, only the intellectual climate that has changed. The sociocultural conditions faced by sociologists have also undergone what certainly seems to be a rapid process of transformation. Integral to this has been the increasingly reflexive nature of contemporary social life, whereby individuals have come to feel a greater sense of responsibility for who they are, and engage in what Giddens (1991) has termed the 'reflexive project of the self'. This has had important implications for our relationships with both our own and, indeed, other people's bodies. The body has increasingly come to be seen as a site on which the subject could 'work' in an effort to construct a sense of self-identity, of difference from those around them. This, combined with the rise of the body in consumer culture as a bearer of symbolic value (see Chapter 4 in this volume), has also led to an explosion in the number of organizations concerned with the maintenance, upkeep and improvement of the body. Weight loss and keep-fit are multimillion dollar industries (Shilling 1993), plastic surgery is one of the fastest-growing areas of medical specialism (K. Davis 1995) and the beauty and cosmetics industry has burgeoned into big business to say the least (Wolf 1990). All of these are industries in which significant numbers of 'working bodies' are employed specifically to work on the bodies of others.

However, these external factors were not in themselves sufficient to revalorize the body in the eyes of sociologists of work. In addition to the above developments, the nature and organization of work had itself also changed during the 1980s. Shifts in the organization of global capitalist economies, the rise of post-Fordist modes of production and exchange, and the demands of an expanding tertiary sector have meant that even greater attention has been paid to issues of image and appearance by organizations concerned with maintaining global competitiveness. Integral to this has been the substantial increase in the proportion of jobs in which people are employed specifically to work as front-line 'customer facing' service providers. This is significant in that it has resulted in a particular emphasis being placed by employers on the body image that workers project and the quality of embodied interactions in the working environment. Under these circumstances, a key component of the work performed by many people has become the presentation, maintenance and performance of a body that is specified by their employing organization. Consequently, sociologists interested in the organization of work have begun to focus more specific attention on the working body than was previously the case. In short, the realization that 'human bodies have to be trained, manipulated, cajoled, coaxed and in general disciplined' (Turner 1992: 15) has become an important theme in the sociological analysis of work.

The working body

> Work. The very word, for many, conjures up a vision of the more or less direct exercise of power upon the body of the worker: coercion, exploitation, discipline, control.
>
> (Rose 1989: 55)

Early systematic studies of work and its organization tended largely to derive from a managerialist concern with problems of efficiency and worker motivation under the demands of industrial capitalism. Industrialization and the expansion of the factory system during the nineteenth century led to new pressures being felt both by those whose labour power was employed directly to produce manufactured goods and also by those who were increasingly responsible for the overseeing and coordination of such activities. As Goldman and Van Houten (1980: 108) have noted, the late eighteenth and early nineteenth centuries were a time when the location of these industrial enterprises was being transformed from 'chaotic and ad-hoc factories to rationalized, well-ordered manufacturing settings'. This introduction of rational modes of organization, based on a world view shaped by the rise of the natural sciences, was to have serious implications not only for how the activity of work itself was organized, but also for the transformation of the body into a labouring machine.

At the forefront of this rationalization process was the work of Frederick Taylor and his system of 'scientific management' (Taylor 1911). Taylor's approach was premised on the idea that there was one best way of organizing any task, and that this could be identified through the close, systematic observation of the task at hand, and its subsequent modification based on these observations. Managers were to be given full responsibility for directing such modified tasks, with workers merely following the instructions and procedures laid down to them. For Taylor, the human body was envisaged as little more than an instrument of labour, a source of effort and skill. The agenda of scientific management was to increase productivity by streamlining and rationalizing production. This was achieved, in part, by intensifying the use of the body as a source of effort and appropriating it as a source of skill. Consequently, the managerial principles of scientific management meant that the working body (as a source of skill) came to be the object of inquiry in order that the human body (as the source of effort) could become the object of more exacting control. Once explicated, the worker's skill could then be appropriated according to management and not worker imperatives.

This dimension of scientific management, the study and appropriation of the worker's body, was perhaps most fully developed in the work of the Gilbreths (1916), who developed the 'motion study'. This involved, through the use of photography, a detailed study of the body performing a particular work task. The motions involved were then broken down into their component elements based on 18 'therbligs', or basic units of movement. The Gilbreths argued that reducing the number of bodily movements to complete a given task would not only increase productivity, it would also reduce the worker's level of bodily fatigue. They argued, however, that such an approach to the problem of fatigue should not be taken in isolation. For example, the need for appropriate rest periods to allow for the regeneration of bodily strength was also an important component of what they were proposing. Thus, it was the rationalization of the workforce's bodies – bodies which, as Burrell (1997) notes, were often viewed as those of little more than dumb animals – that exemplified many of the early attempts at managerial intervention into the world of industrialized labour.

The idea that the body could, and indeed should, be viewed as little more than a labouring machine, ripe for the attention of those efficiency experts pursuing rationalization, was also acknowledged by those working outside of the sphere of early twentieth-century managerial planning. In his critical analysis of the rise of the bureaucratic mode of organization, Weber (1968 [1921]) noted that the rationalization and disciplining of the body was central to the successful operation of modern factory-based manufacturing systems. It was in this context that he observed that:

> The psycho-physical apparatus of man is completely adjusted to the demands of the outer world, the tools, the machines – in short, it is functionalized, and the individual is shorn of his natural rhythm as determined by his organism; in line with the demands of the work procedure, he is attuned to a new rhythm through the functional specialization of muscles and through the creation of an optimal economy of physical effort.
>
> (Weber 1968: 1156)

The working body, then, as with all other aspects of human life was, in Weber's view, increasingly falling under the sway of the indomitable logic of rationalization: a logic that he believed would eventually subsume 'modern' civilization.

Returning briefly to the development of managerial thinking during the early twentieth century, however, it did seem that by the 1930s a shift in emphasis was starting to take place. Management theorists concerned with improving levels of productivity and efficiency were still preoccupied with the body as a tool of labour. However, the emphasis had started to gravitate more towards the need to win the 'minds' of the labour force rather than to discipline and regulate their bodies exclusively. Ironically, one of the reasons for this shift of managerial emphasis was the unexpected result of the now somewhat infamous studies undertaken during the 1930s at the Hawthorne Works of the Western Electrical Company. There, a team of industrial researchers initially set out to study the effects of changing illumination patterns on the worker. As such, their original concerns were closely, although not entirely, allied to the issues of bodily fatigue that were, in part, characteristic of the model of scientific management outlined above. However, the interpretation and presentation of the findings of the Hawthorne Studies, most notably by Mayo (1933) and Roethlisberger and Dickson (1939), led to an increased awareness among managers of the psychological and interpersonal dimensions of the work experience. This development was also fuelled by the growth, during the period between the

First and Second World Wars, of what became known as 'industrial psychology' (see Rose 1989). As the title suggests, this approach tended to focus on the refinement of the worker's psyche as the key means of motivating the worker to achieve greater levels of output, rather than by the direct disciplining of the body. This hierarchical model of the relationship between mind and body can be seen in the work of two of the most influential figures in this field, Maslow (1958) and Herzberg (1968). For Maslow, a humanist psychologist, the key to motivation was an understanding that human beings have a 'hierarchy of needs', and each level of needs must be met in order to progress to the next level. Herzberg, who was more directly concerned with worker motivation, argued that two types of factors must be taken into account when managers talk about motivating their employees, the first being what he termed hygiene factors, the second being motivation factors. The important point here, however, is that for both men, what they considered to be lower order factors – that is, basic needs in Maslow's case and hygiene factors in Herzberg's – largely comprised of physiological elements. As such, it was prescribed from the 1930s onwards that the higher needs and therefore the 'real' concerns of managers should be those of the psychological well-being of the employee rather than the crude physiological ergonomics associated with scientific management.

Generally speaking, early sociological studies of work and its organization followed this managerial tendency towards marginalizing the issue of the body at work. Indeed, in many respects, the body (itself the object of rationalization) found itself rationalized out of the picture. It was viewed as having little to do with the clean and sanitized world of the work organization or, indeed, sociology itself. This absence of the body in the sociology of work can thus be seen, in part, as the outcome of a deliberate attempt at silencing that which was deemed to fall outside of the concerns of rational social science. The body as a pre-social given was seen as the concern not of social but of natural science, even in the workplace. Yet despite this, through critical accounts of the workplace the material presence of the body continued to assert its presence. An example of this can be found in Braverman's (1974) Marxist critique of the continuing importance of scientific management to the capitalist labour process. Braverman argued that the Taylorist emphasis on the 'deskilling of work' – the stripping of each task down to its simplest components, reducing discretion and the routinization of work activities – created tangible processes that operated on the bodies of workers, organizing and directing their every action. For Braverman, the introduction and popularization of the moving assembly line represented a triumph of what Marx referred to as 'dead labour over living labour' (cited in Braverman 1974: 228), one that removed the last vestiges of control the living worker has over the labour process. Technology, then, under the conditions of industrial capitalism, serves, in Braverman's reading at least, not to ease the burden of labour on the human body but rather to extend managerial control over the bodies of the labour force.

Indeed, common to most sociological accounts that have touched on the relationship between work and the body is a deep-seated unease about the impact that technologies have on the bodily dimension of human life. At best, technological development has been read by some sociologists as a double-edged sword. Shilling (1993: 3; emphasis in original), for example, notes how, at one and the same time, technology generally has 'advanced the potential many people have to control their own bodies *and* to have them controlled by others'. This is particularly true of industrial technology which, on the one hand, has the potential to free the production process from the organic limits of the body and to diminish 'the most painful forms of exertion associated with the work of making things' (Zuboff 1988: 30). On the other hand, however, industrial technology also restricts opportunities to accrue knowledge and skill in the labour process (Braverman 1974) *and* has facilitated the growth of systems of industrial governance that depend, increasingly it seems, on the rationalization and control of the body. As such, technology, especially when in the service of the capitalist pursuit of profit, is viewed as a means through which the process of rationalization can once again be extended into the fibres of the living body and so, too, into the minds of employees.

Not that all commentators are quite as pessimistic as this, however. For example, in their recent account of the relationship between the working body and technology, Parker and Cooper (1998) draw on the popular image of the cyborg in science fiction in an attempt to reconceptualize this relationship. For them we are all, in one way or another, part of a form of 'cyberorganization'; one in which human organs are inexorably intertwined with non-human artefacts. These artefacts can include the most simple of things, such as desks, pens or even coffee machines. The point is, however, that the patterns of ordered activity that we define as organizations are the outcomes of our interactions as bodies with such non-human components. Indeed, for Parker and Cooper, organizations and the roles we play in them could not come into being without such interactions, which challenge the traditional bifurcation of 'wo/man' and 'machine'. As they put it, 'this surely means that meat and metal are not that radically different. We couldn't *do* "manager", "academic", "reader" or "cinema audience" if it wasn't for all the various props and accessories that allow us to perform such roles' (Parker and Cooper 1998: 209; emphasis in original). In their analysis we are all cyborgs – that is, temporary assemblages of bodies and things the moment we undertake an organ-izational task, conjoined in a relationship of body and technology that is not so much one of repressive rationalization but one of mutual enablement.

This account of the cyborg relationship between the body and externalized artefacts can in part be seen as a manifestation of the postmodern concern to undermine the dualist structures that Enlightenment-inspired modes of thinking have tended to rely on. In this case, it is the duality of human flesh and non-human objects that Parker and

Cooper challenge. A similar version of this argument can be found in Barry and Hazen's (1996) attempt to reconceptualize the body at work from a self-avowedly postmodernist perspective. For them, the collapse of the modernist vision of the unified subject opens up new opportunities to dissolve previous boundaries between externalized organizational forms and the embodied sense of self, which in turn could lead to new ways of understanding the relationship humans have with the organizations they have created:

> We suggest . . . that as we stop seeing our selves in modernist terms, as rational, egocentric, goal driven creatures, and begin to experience our selves as energy flows, with fluid boundaries and multiple realities, our organizational images and theories can change as well.
> (Barry and Hazen 1996: 153)

Although the impact of a postmodern-inspired anti-dualism has played a significant role in the move to re-establish the body as a concern for sociologists of work and organization, few have taken their conclusions to such an extreme; however, most approaches inspired by postmodernism have tended to re-emphasize critically the process of rationalization and eventual obfuscation the body has undergone in the workplace. For example, in his study of the relationship between sexuality and work, Gibson Burrell (1984) has the Cadbury Village of Bournville in the UK and Ford's Detroit-based Sociological Department in the USA both representing serious attempts to create 'total institutions' around the body of the worker. Such organizations, he notes, were designed particularly to repress the hedonistic proclivities of bodily passions. More recently, in his attempt to develop what he terms a 'retro-organization theory', Burrell (1997: 47) has called for an exploration of the irrational underside of organizational life in which 'the visceral, the carnal, the bodily, the unclean can come to the focus of attention'. Such a focus, he argues, would provide a challenge to what he considers to be an ideology of rationality and objectivity underpinning organizational power and, indeed, its analysis.

In this respect, a significant influence on Burrell's work (see, for example, Burrell 1988 and 1997) has been the writing of the post-structuralist theorist Michel Foucault. Foucault's (1977 and 1978) concepts of 'bio-power' and 'discipline' have also been appropriated and deployed by a number of other social scientists concerned with questions of organizational power and the mechanisms through which power is operationalized. In Foucault's work, the concept of 'bio-power' is used to describe the ways in which the body is subjugated through various techniques of surveillance and organization. The related concept of 'discipline' describes the process by which such techniques produce a state of internalized compliance with the demands of external authority and control. In the study of work organizations, both of these concepts have been deployed in analyses of those demands, which are increasingly placed on employees, by the introduction of flexible working patterns and total quality systems associated with what have been termed 'post-Fordist' (Amin 1994) modes of production and distribution. Barbara Townley (1994), for example, draws on Foucault to argue that the discourse and practices associated with Human Resource Management (HRM) serve to provide managers with the necessary resources to locate and transform employee subjectivity, in part through the embodied dimension of an individual's sense of self. This in turn helps to produce more flexible and responsive employees, who are willing and able to meet the demands of new forms of work organization. Hopper and Macintosh (1998) similarly deploy the work of Foucault in a comparative analysis of management control systems, in which common practices such as timetabling and hierarchical surveillance are understood as means by which employees' bodies are ordered and trained in relation to the 'apparatus of production'.

A key aspect of Foucault's conception of disciplinary power deployed in these studies is the analysis of various forms of surveillance. Using the term 'panopticism', Foucault (1977) adapts Jeremy Bentham's (1995 [1791]) account of a panoptic prison design to describe the technique of unseen surveillance used in the maintenance of discipline in modern organizations. Foucault's concept of panopticism also feeds into recent accounts of workplace control techniques and has inspired a number of studies into the ways in which employees' bodies have become subject to technologies of rationalization and control as key sites of surveillance. Such accounts have emphasized particularly the evolution of a 'technological panopticon' as a consequence of relatively recent developments in information technology in the workplace (Sewell and Wilkinson 1992; Steingard and Fitzgibbons 1993). Hollway (1984) has also highlighted the extent to which the use of chemical tests for alcohol and drug use, as well as a range of viruses, enables corporate 'experts' in attitudes and bodily fluids to assess the purity of employees. Such critical accounts have continued to emphasize the ways in which the human body acts as a site of rationalization, where values of efficiency and productivity continue to provide the guiding logic of intervention.

In a continuation of this concern with the rationalization of working bodies, sociologists have also recently started to draw attention to the processes through which not only the worker's embodied labour power (their effort and skills) but also their body image is incorporated into organizational life. Something of an analytical shift in sociological approaches to the working body – away from the organic body as an instrument of labour and towards more of an emphasis on the body as the bearer of symbolic value – can be identified. This analytical shift means that attention has been given, relatively recently, to the various ways in which work organizations seek to represent themselves in and through the bodies of their employees. Recent research has focused, for instance, on the ways in which organizations strive to assume a collective, corporate (corporeal) identity through the cultivation of 'organizational bodies' (see Hassard et al. 2000).

Adopting such a focus in their work on organizational dress, Rafaeli and Pratt (1993), for example, have highlighted the ways in which attributes of dress carry valuable symbolic information. Health service personnel, for instance, tend to wear white to convey purity and cleanliness, while police and security services use dark colours to convey power and authority. As such, the bodies of organizational employees are themselves the carriers of values deemed concomitant with the ethos of the organizations by which they are employed. More generally, then, formal dress is associated with being 'professional' because of repeated exposure to professional people wearing suits. Thus, individuals wearing suits might come to be perceived as professional. When employees of an organization wear suits, therefore, the associations triggered by these attributes may affect the organization itself, such that if employees wear suits, the organization itself may be perceived as professional. Similarly, uniformity of dress tends to be regarded as an indication of what is often a core value in organizations that specialize in mass production of services, namely consistency. Kroc (1977), the Chief Executive Officer of McDonald's, adopted this logic for example, when he demanded that employees of the McDonald's fast food chain maintain strictly uniform standards of organizational dress. In contrast, organizations such as Macintosh Computers, which claim to endorse creativity and innovation, often eschew homogeneous dress as a means of conveying such organizational values. Rafaeli and Pratt (1993) also note the extent to which organizational dress is frequently gender-based. Suits, for example, are formal and convey traits that are traditionally perceived as 'masculine'. In this respect, female managers may choose to 'power dress', aping male styles in dress and demeanour and so evoking masculine power. As such, Rafaeli and Pratt (1993) emphasize the extent to which dress is an active agent in the production of working bodies, in so far as it may help to bring about employee compliance and legitimation of a particular organizational image or value system.

In the case of service work in particular, sociology has increasingly highlighted how the management of organizational bodies seems to be concerned with the body as the material signifier of the values of an employing organization. Van Maanen (1991) uses the term 'smile factories' to describe theme parks and their staged performances. In the 'show' metaphor, which characterizes leisure organizations such as the Disney Corporation, employees are 'cast members' who wear 'costumes' (not uniforms), playing their 'roles' (not working) to 'guests' (not consumers). As Boje (1995: 1016) has put it, 'in sum, Disney sustains the modernist production machine to turn images into commodities for mass consumption while cloaking employees in a storybook role as smiling performers in a show'. This mode of analysis is taken a step further by Hancock and Tyler (2000), who have argued, drawing on the work of Gagliardi (1996), that female flight attendants' bodies are groomed and manipulated, through the use of make-up, dress and regimes of dieting, to represent not only an organizational ethos but also a pathos – that is, an aesthetic, sensate experience their employing airline wishes to convey to its clients. Thus, they become embodied artefacts, projecting through their physical appearance the glamour and beauty that the airline's management wish the organization to be associated with. However, feminist accounts have noted that, although often given an appearance of 'naturalness', the maintenance of 'organizational bodies' usually demands hard work (Bartky 1990; Adkins 1995; Tyler and Abbott 1998).

A similar set of issues has also been identified in relation to what has been termed 'emotional labour'. Following Hochschild (1983), 'emotional labour' refers to the management of human feelings, sensations and affective responses in the capitalist labour process 'to create a publicly observable facial and bodily display' (Hochschild 1983: 7). In the performance of emotional labour, therefore, 'one's face and one's feelings take on the property of a resource . . . to be used to make money' (Hochschild 1983: 55). In an organizational environment of intensifying global competition, how a service is delivered has come to be perceived as central to overall organizational success. As a result, those employees who operate particularly as 'front line' service providers, and are thus perceived as key representatives of their organization, have become the focus of considerable organizational intervention into almost every aspect of their presentation of self. As Noon and Blyton (1997: 128) have noted, 'customer-facing staff are situated in crucial "boundary-spanning" positions which link the organization to external individuals or groups'. The successful performance of emotional labour – pulling off a good act – typically requires 'a complex combination of facial expression, body language, spoken words and tone of voice' (Rafaeli and Sutton 1987: 33). This combination often is secured and maintained through processes of selection, training, supervision and monitoring of employee presentation and performance (Leidner 1993; Tyler and Abbott 1998), frequently involving techniques of employee peer and self-surveillance. Even in call centres, the fastest-expanding sector of the UK economy at the beginning of the twenty-first century, employees are instructed to use their tone of voice to compensate for the lack of face-to-face contact with customers and to 'sell' their organization (Taylor and Bain 1998).

With regard to the gendered relationship between bodies and the performance of emotional labour, although sociology has emphasized that a number of people are required increasingly to manage their bodies in a wide range of working environments, 'there are aspects which appear to be specific to a milieu in which women are in the front line providing a service to predominantly male customers' (Filby 1992: 36). In this sense, emotional labour, and the embodied performance it demands, is understood by sociologists to be defined largely according to the skills and abilities that women are deemed to possess by virtue of their perceived 'nature' or essence. Thus, perhaps one of the most striking aspects of the contemporary organization of the body in and through work is that it creates the impression that gender differences in personality, interests, character, appearance, manner and competence are natural. Recent sociological accounts of the relationship between work and the body, particularly those influenced by contemporary feminist theory, have thus highlighted the importance of gender as an aspect of social identity that shapes this relationship.

Gendered bodies at work

Recent feminist analyses have focused on the control of women's bodies and the gendered organization of work as intimately connected. In particular, feminist sociology has focused on gender differences in the role and management of the body at work. Cockburn (1991) has alerted us to a politics of bodies in the workplace, and Hearn and Parkin (1995: 20) have argued that the management of the dialectical relationship that is 'organization sexuality' is based largely on 'precision in the control of the body'. Similarly, in a recent critique of the film *Disclosure* (1994), Brewis (1998) emphasizes the extent to which the lead female character is reduced largely to her sexualized body. Empirical studies of so-called 'women's work' have also identified several examples of occupations, such as nursing (James 1989), secretarial work (Pringle 1989) and waitressing and bar work (Hall 1993; Adkins 1995), in which certain properties, qualities and attributes associated with women's bodies are commodified. Much of this feminist research stands in stark contrast to the emphasis on labouring males in traditional, industrial sociology which, as Wray-Bliss and Parker (1998) have noted, tends towards a heroization of 'work hardened bodies' and of masculine values of strength and muscularity.

The extent to which women continue to be the prime servicers of men's 'work hardened' bodies has been highlighted by feminists, as has the commodification of women's bodies in pornography, prostitution and surrogate motherhood (Pateman 1988). A number of feminists have also focused on the implications of women's care of men's and children's bodies for women's relatively disadvantaged position in the labour markets of western societies (Hartmann 1979; Walby 1990). Others have highlighted the potential effects of workplace hazards on women's reproductive health, focusing on complex issues such as fetal protection policies and their impact on employment opportunities for women (Norton 1996). Orbach (1986) has focused on compulsive eating as a consequence of women's social oppression, arguing that the restricted labour market opportunities available to women are one of the main forces that distort women's bodily development, causing women to regard themselves as commodities whose value is based only on body image.

In this sense, feminist sociologists have noted that Giddens' (1991: 219) aforementioned understanding of the body as an integral element of the 'reflexive project of the self' seriously underestimates the extent to which women's bodies as 'projects' – particularly the bodies of women workers – continue to be more reflective of patriarchal norms and instrumentally imposed aesthetic codes, than expressions of a self-determined individuality (Tyler and Abbott 1998). Thus, while some feminists have rejected Foucault's work on the body as 'blind to those disciplines that produce a modality of embodiment that is peculiarly feminine' (McNay 1992: 89), others have drawn on his concept of 'docile bodies' to argue that '. . . in so far as the disciplinary practices of femininity produce a subjected and practised . . . body, they must be understood as aspects of a far larger discipline, an oppressive and inegalitarian system of sexual subordination' (Bartky 1990: 71).

What feminist research has highlighted, then, is the extent to which women, in a number of disparate roles and in a variety of occupational and organizational settings, are classified and utilized specifically for their bodies. In advertising and marketing, goods, services and the organizations that provide them are made attractive and 'sexy' because the women used to advertise them are sexually attractive; the 'quality' of the service and of the organization itself is guaranteed by their sexualized bodies. In this sense, the 'figures, the personality and the bums' are all increasingly important commercially (Filby 1992: 23). In a whole range of servicing occupations, women are employed for their sexually attractive bodies. Indeed, as Scott and Morgan (1993: 16) note, bodies are not distributed randomly throughout work organizations. The practice of locating 'attractive' women at frontstage areas such as reception desks is a clear indication of the interplay between gender, body image and power within work organizations. In this respect, eating disorders, referred to by Shilling (1993: 92) as an expression of the 'breakdown of the body under the competitive pressures of self-presentation', have been linked with the demands of certain types of 'feminized' work that require women to conform to gendered regulations governing the size, shape and overall presentation of their bodies (Tyler and Abbott 1998). Such accounts are not limited to the engendering of female bodies however. For example, focusing on the demands of masculinity in his ethnographic account of the work of professional boxers, Wacquant (1993: 90; emphasis in original) highlights the extent to which 'the bodily labour of fighters is fundamentally a work of *engenderment* in the sense that it creates a new being but also a gendered being embodying and exemplifying a definite form of masculinity: plebeian, heterosexual, and heroic'.

Body work

So far in this chapter, we have focused particularly on the role of the body in remunerated employment in formal, work organizations. In concentrating on the body in paid work, our account thus far has tended simply to reflect the focus of most sociological analyses of the relationship between the body and work. However, in this penultimate section we consider an important yet neglected aspect of the working body, namely the work that we all do on our bodies in the context of our everyday lives. As Shilling notes (1993: 118), 'body work is rarely called work, but in cleaning our teeth, washing our bodies, cutting our nails, making-up, or shaving our legs or faces, we are all working on our bodies'. The term 'body work' is used here, then, to refer to the work that is carried out on the body outside of the formal domain of wage labour yet which is central to the maintenance of working bodies and which continues to be a relatively marginal concern of the sociological analysis of the relationship between the body and work. Underpinning this concept of 'body work' is a perception of the body 'as an entity that is in a constant process of becoming; a *project* which should be worked at and accomplished as part of an *individual's* self-identity' (Shilling 1993: 5; emphasis in original). The pursuit of the body as a perpetually unfinished project thus involves

> individuals being conscious of and actively concerned about the *management*, maintenance and appearance of their bodies . . . both as personal resources and as social symbols which give off messages about a person's self-identity. In this context, bodies become malleable entities which can be shaped and honed by the vigilance and *hard work* of their owners.
>
> (Shilling 1993: 5; emphasis added)

The basis of body work as Shilling understands it, therefore, is 'an implicit ontology of the body which highlights its status as an unfinished phenomenon . . . an entity which can be "completed" only through human labour' (Shilling 1993: 124–5).

Pierre Bourdieu's (1984) analysis of the body as 'physical capital', as the bearer of power, status and distinction which is integral to the accumulation of various resources, is particularly useful to a sociological analysis of body work and its organization, in this respect. Bourdieu's conceptualization of the body as a form of physical capital highlights the commodification of the body and the management of the body as central to the acquisition of status and 'distinction'. He recognizes that acts of labour are required to transform bodies into social entities and that these acts influence how people develop their bodies. Far from being natural, these acts of labour 'represent highly skilled and socially differentiated accomplishments' (Shilling 1993: 128). In particular, Bourdieu's account provides a useful framework within which to understand the relationship between production and consumption and the ways in which this relationship is related in and through body work. For instance, as we noted earlier, the management and moulding of the body has become increasingly central to the labour markets of contemporary western societies, and this has taken place within the commercial context of a growing industry catering for the demands of body work (Featherstone 1991b).

According to Bourdieu (1984), bodies bear the imprint of society as a consequence of three main factors: (i) social location (the material circumstances that shape everyday life and that constrain the development of the body); (ii) habitus (acquired social skills, such as ability in presenting and performing the body); and (iii) taste (according to which individuals appropriate as voluntary choices and preferences, lifestyles and cultural dispositions that are shaped materially). In Bourdieu's account, bodies develop through the interrelation between an individual's social location, their habitus and taste, which serve to shape the body as a marker of 'distinction'. This interrelation locates the body in what he terms a 'body schema' (Bourdieu 1984: 218), a hierarchical network of bodies organized according to social status.

As Shilling notes (1993: 132–3), although Bourdieu does not provide a detailed account of the gendered aspects of body work, his analysis can be extended to take account of gender as well as other aspects of social identity and, particularly, of the ways in which social differences are 'naturalized'; that is, made to seem as if they were the outcome of a pre-social nature. This naturalization of body work is important to Bourdieu's general theory of social reproduction as he sees that there are substantial inequalities in the symbolic values accorded to particular bodily forms, as realized, for instance, in the labour market.

To summarize Bourdieu's account of body work, social location is understood to exert a fundamental influence on the ways in which bodies develop and on the symbolic (and material) values accorded to particular bodily forms; hence the reproduction of bodies as physical capital. Central to the value of different forms of physical capital and to their valorization is the ability of dominant groups to define their bodies and lifestyles as superior, worthy of reward and as 'the embodiment of class' (Shilling 1993: 140). Sociologists have argued, then, that the very process of working through the body has come to be seen as part of a complex of behaviours distinguishing the civilized from the less civilized (Elias 1978). To maintain a certain distance from one's own body, and especially from those of others, has developed as an important sign of hierarchical position in western societies manifest not least in the workplace. Various aspects of social identity, such as gender and social class, race and ethnicity, age, sexuality and disability, shape such embodied hierarchies, as the body acts as an important bearer of value in contemporary social, cultural and labour markets.

Conclusion

There is considerable evidence of a reinvigorated sociological interest in the body and work, which this chapter has aimed, within its relatively limited space, to review and reflect on. As we have noted, however, the idea that the body has ever been truly absent from work and its study is a misleading one. The body has, at least following the rise of industrial capitalism, been understood as something that requires taming and rationalizing if the organization of work is to follow the path of efficiency and productivity that capitalism demands of it. What recent developments in both the discipline of sociology and the world of work have done is made more explicit the ways in which the body is the object of increasingly sophisticated and pervasive technologies of rationalization. Such technologies function to harness the body's capacity both for labour and for symbolic expression, while simultaneously attempting to neutralize it as a source of disorder and irrationality.

We would suggest that a more critical understanding of the appropriation of the body as an instrument of labour and also, increasingly it seems, as a signifier of particular work organizations would provide at least a basis for the continued development of this area of research. Much recent sociological analysis has tended to focus on representations of the body in consumer culture and this has, in large part, been at the expense of developing a critical sociological account of the body at work and of the nature and extent of body work involved in the production and reproduction of working bodies. It would seem, to us at least, that such a critical understanding could do worse than begin by considering Bourdieu's (1984) approach to the body as a marker of 'distinction' and Shilling's (1993) conceptualization of 'body work' that we have considered at the end of the chapter.

Further reading

As we have already noted, there are comparatively few texts that concern themselves specifically with the relationship between the body and the organization of work. One recently published collection which does deal directly with this relationship, however, is *Body and Organization* (2000) edited by Hassard, Holliday and Willmott, and which provides a broad overview of much of the current thinking in the field. Several essays in *Organization Representation* (1998), also edited by Hassard and Holliday, are equally worth looking at, especially those concerned with gender and organizational representation. Gibson Burrell's somewhat surreal attempt to develop an alternative and certainly non-instrumentalist mode of organization theorizing, *Pandemonium* (1997), is worth consulting in terms of its evocation of the role organization has always played in the ordering and repression of the corporeal dimension of everyday life. For those particularly interested in the contribution of Foucauldian scholarship to organizational studies, especially in terms of the status of the body in relation to technologies of control, then Michel Foucault's own account of the growth of a 'disciplinary society', *Discipline and Punish* (1977), is as good, and, indeed, as gory a place to start as any. In addition to this, *Foucault,*

Management and Organization Theory (1997), a collection edited by McKinlay and Starkey, contains some insightful contributions. A number of broadly feminist writers who touch on the relationship between work and the gendered body are worth exploring, most notably perhaps Lisa Adkins' study of female employees in the hospitality industry, *Gendered Work* (1995), and Jeff Hearn and Wendy Parkin's *'Sex' at 'Work'* (1995), the title of which amply indicates its concerns. For those interested in a selection of the 'classics' of work and organization theory, including those alluded to in the opening section of this chapter, then Clark, Chandler and Barry's impressive collection of readings by leading writers in the field, entitled *Organizations and Identities* (1994), is a must. Those seeking a more advanced theoretical analysis should consult Karen Dale's (2000) 'Under The Knife', which explores the relationship between the body, contemporary social theory and organizations. Finally, several leading journals in work and organization studies are certainly worth consulting in this respect, most notably *Gender, Work and Organization, Organization* and *Work, Employment and Society*.

CHAPTER 6

Ethical bodies

RACHEL RUSSELL

Introduction

Ethics in modernity was founded on reason, on the idea that universal rules of conduct could and should be embedded in social life. With the advent of postmodernity, it has been argued that this project has come apart at the seams and that we live in a society without obligations. Bauman (1993: 3) rejects this perspective. He argues that the jury is still out and that we cannot yet tell whether or not 'postmodernity will go down in history as the twilight or the renaissance of morality'. Certainly, the idea that we have entered a post-deontic or post-ethical era does not fit well with either the general proliferation of (sociological) debate about ethics or the specific process by which embodiment is being drawn into it. This claim does not suggest a renaissance either but it does delineate the content of this chapter, which will attempt to situate the new prominence of the body in society and in sociology in the context of the re-emergence of the 'moral'. Despite the growing influence of the moral and the corporeal in sociological discourse, the 'ethical body' remains relatively unexplored terrain.

The rapidly expanding corpus of knowledge that is now referred to as the sociology of the body is well known for presenting accounts of both the various ways in which the body is fashioned in contemporary culture and the ways in which our different experiences of this culture are invariably embodied (Smart 1996). However, in the rather broad remit generated by the multifarious ways in which sociologists have sought to address the nature and significance of bodies, little attention has been paid to the 'ethical body' (Smart 1996) or to the ways in which the body 'figures' in constructions of ethical identity. What the literature neglects, therefore, is an embodied conception of ethics. However, the ethical and somatic revivals in society (embodied linguistically in the new 'discipline' of bioethics) and sociology are both represented in current debates in sociological theory. This chapter will begin by addressing this convergence. It will then go on to use it as a point of departure to analyse the ways in which the contemporary interplay between ethics and embodiment reflects wider cultural processes in which sensuality and the affects are establishing themselves as important sources of 'value'.

The body figures in moral considerations as both a generator of ethical issues and as a site for embodied ethics. With respect to the former, examples are legion. Surrogate motherhood, prenatal genetic screening, abortion, euthanasia, cosmetic surgery and transsexuality are just a few of the issues that animate contemporary bioethical debate (Gillon 1994). However, the focus of this discussion will not be on ethical 'issues' per se, but rather on the ways in which the body 'lives' ethics. The body has come to be seen as the site of ethical identity and it is this particular rapprochement between the moral and the somatic that will command attention.

The idea of the ethical body or the notion of the body as a site for the embodiment of ethics raises the question of the relationship between ethics and aesthetics. Eagleton (1990: 13) notes that the concept of the aesthetic arises out of eighteenth-century discourse on the body. The collision of aesthetics and ethics is not new. Greek and Judaic-Christian thought as well as Kantian philosophy contain traces of it. Yet this form of embodied ethics has come alive once again in contemporary consumer culture and is very evident in popular culture and daily language (Synnott 1993), so much so that Featherstone (1995) and Welsch (1997) draw attention to a process that they call the 'aestheticization of everyday life'. Important contemporary thinkers such as Foucault (1997) and Maffesoli (1996) have also made contributions to the debate about the postmodern liaison between aesthetics and ethics. The idea that ethics can be understood as an 'art of existence' (Foucault 1997) suggests that the ethical can be identified in the embodied practices of everyday life. Such an approach questions the modernist notion in which ethics is reduced to a universal rational code that is socially administered to regulate desire and tame the unpredictable nature of embodiment. Contemporary writers such as Bauman (1993) and Irigaray (1993) – drawing heavily on the work of Emmanuel Levinas (1981) – highlight the emotional and sensual aspects of ethical bodies. Levinas (1981) conceptualizes embodied ethics as an ethics of responsibility, and those who reject the modernist view of the body as 'otherness' find his philosophy fertile ground for sowing the seeds of a sociology of embodied ethics.

Theories/ethics/bodies

The implicit convergence of the moral and the body in sociology suggests the concept of the 'ethical body'. The two elements that constitute the concept share some historical similarities in the sociological canon. Although sociology is now aware of what Shilling (1993) refers to as the body's 'absent presence' in its own tradition, it is less aware of this 'peculiarity' in relation to the moral. Shilling (1993: 9) reminds us that the resurfacing of the body in sociology is linked to the sinking of the intellect. As the mind has relinquished its dominant position in the mind–body partnership, the corporeal has moved into the limelight. In a similar vein, ethics is winning its autonomy from reason and beginning to emerge from its contemporary relationship with aesthetics as a sociological domain with a distinct identity. Yet although the 'founding fathers' of sociology were reticent in facing up to the corporeal they were vehement in voicing their moral concerns. However, they were concerned more with developing an ethical sociology than a sociology of ethics.

Steven Seidman (1998: 11), in his recent attempt to revitalize social theory by arguing for a return to its role as 'a morally significant public practice', makes this point quite forcibly. A moral agenda for social theory would be a return rather than a new departure. He draws attention to Comte's passionate reaction to the cultural disorder of post-revolutionary France. It became a call for a new science of society that he called sociology. Comte argued that sociology was capable of demonstrating scientifically the processes that bring order to chaos. For Comte, scientific authority was the solution to the demise of clerical autocratic authority. Mainstream sociology (from its early adherence to and later critique of positivism and scientism) tended to lose sight of what Delanty (1997: 26) refers to as 'the positivistic heritage of moralistic reformism'. Comte's moral vision and motivation tend to 'burst through' the scientific discourse to reveal sociologists as the new 'high priests of the positive society' (Seidman 1998: 31). Charles Lemert's (1995) *Sociology after the Crisis* tells a similar story with respect to Durkheim's ambitious attempt to organize Comte's new science into an academic discipline. Durkheim's (1984 [1893]) *The Division of Labour in Society*, argues Lemert (1995: 22), 'was as much a moral philosophy as a sociology'. Durkheim intended sociology to act in accordance with principles of moral order. His work displayed an intense concern with the connections between the moral and the social.

Comte and Durkheim were not the only 'classical' theorists to have demonstrated the centrality of moral commitment to both sociology and society. Similar cases can be made for Marx and Weber (Lemert 1995; Seidman 1998). Notwithstanding the scientific pretensions of classical sociological theory, the 'founding fathers' were – to a man – in pursuit of moral order. As Lemert (1995: xv) reminds us, 'Sociology was founded by a generation of thinkers who cared very much for sociology . . . because they cared deeply about the world as a whole'. The contemporary backlash against scientific versions of sociology makes it easy to forget that for these early thinkers, a scientific theory of society was conceived as a profoundly liberating force, a means of progressing beyond ignorance and want by providing legitimation for a new secular authority that would enlighten humankind.

Periodically, as Lemert (1995) and Seidman (1998) acknowledge, sociological theorists have attempted to remind sociologists of their moral role. These reminders include C. Wright Mills' classic critique of 1959 and Alvin Gouldner's (1971) 'crisis' call for a reflexive sociology. Contemporary arguments for a reflexive, interpretative sociology of postmodernism (Bauman 1987) are part of the same tradition. Mills (1967 [1959]: 90) argued that, 'Whether he wants it or not, or whether he is aware of it or not, anyone who spends his life studying society and publishing the results is acting morally and usually politically as well'. This claim underpins his argument that sociology lacks imagination. It fails to provide people with adequate explanations of their social world. It does not articulate what ordinary people find pressing and important. Gouldner (1971) argued that sociological theory did not respond to the needs of new social movements. There were, therefore, large numbers of people to whom sociology was superfluous.

However, although the credentials of sociology as a moral agenda have not always been impressive, Lemert (1995) and Seidman (1998) have attempted to revise the history of sociological theory in terms of its engagement with moral issues. They argue that their position is made possible by feminist and postmodern critiques of sociological rationalism and the production of new social knowledge that has been generated by new social movements. Such debates, however, not only underpin the quest for an ethical sociology but have also influenced the development of a sociology of ethics. As Lash (1996: 75) argues, 'ethical debates have become so central in recent years to social and cultural theory that they can no longer be ignored'. Meanwhile, Shilling (1993) has attempted to re-read sociological theory as an excursus on the body. Furthermore, the body has become an issue for sociology in the context of feminist, poststructuralist and phenomenological challenges to the dominance of Cartesian rationalism and the growing importance of the somatic to the social (Turner 1996). One might argue that the marriage between ethics and bodies in the sociological tradition is about to be announced.

However, the engagement between ethics and the body has, to date, been encumbered by one outstanding problem, which has to do with its eclectic theoretical lineage. We are all aware of particular conceptions of ethics that guide laws and seek to regulate bodies and bodily practices. These range from the incorporation of certain Judaic-Christian commandments into legal systems, such as 'thou shalt not kill', to the highly complex policies and legal protocols that control and constrain sexual, reproductive and medical behaviour. However, there is a difference between theorizing the effects on the body of

these socially administered ethical regimes and a theoretical consideration of embodied ethics. These theoretical considerations and embodied
ethics unite in post-Cartesian social theory, but in this broad frame
of reference there is a debate that can be summarized by the following question: Is the body in embodied ethics discursive or fleshy?
Poststructuralist accounts of the body tend to eliminate the fleshy,
material body in favour of one that is discursively produced (Turner
1996; Williams and Bendelow 1998b). Poststructuralism has done
much to put the body on the sociological map. The body is central
to Foucault's account of the relation between power and knowledge
and to his work on the constitution of the 'moral subject' (Falk 1994).
However, because Foucault's focus was on the body as the discursively
ordered and disciplined product of certain forms of institutionalized knowledge, his analysis tends to eclipse the importance of pre-
discursive physicality. As Williams and Bendelow (1998a: 104) point
out, a lot of contemporary sociological reflection on the body has
tended to be 'about rather than from bodies' and has tended to
stress 'representational (i.e. social constructionist) over experiential
(i.e. existential/phenomenological) issues'. One can apply this concern
to 'corporeal feminism' in general (Grosz 1994) and its application
to ethics in particular (Diprose 1994; Shildrick 1997). Shildrick (1997),
for example, examines the ways in which women in modern western
– especially medical – discourse are excluded from the possibility
of realizing both autonomous embodiment and moral personhood.
Yet the phenomenological body as simultaneously subject and object
(Crossley 1995) of ethical action tends to become marginalized by
the uninhibited anti-essentialism that pervades the analytical strategy
of corporeal feminism. This is not a problem that this chapter can
even begin to solve, but it serves to highlight the fact that the story of
theories, ethics and bodies is unfinished. However, one might argue,
tentatively, that the bifurcation between poststructuralist and exist-
entialist approaches to (embodied) ethics is being closed by the work
of Levinas (1981), Bauman (1993, 1994, 1995, 1996) and Irigaray
(1993).

Ethical bodies

The neglect of the ethical body in the more general sociological
'return to the body' (Smart 1996) is surprising given that ethical
issues (more often than not) take shape in response to biopolitical or
biomedical developments, such as those associated with reproductive
and genetic technologies (Steinberg 1997) or those that arise out of
an engagement with the moralization of contemporary health and
welfare discourse, in which disease is often reduced to individual
responsibility (see Chapter 2). Turner's (1996: 6) claim that we live in
a 'somatic society', a society whose significance lies in the fact that

'moral problems are expressed through the conduit of the body', embodies a plethora of implications that are to be addressed.

Turner's (1996) use of the term somatic indicates a new type of emphasis on the body. It is intended to draw our attention to the corporeal or material body rather than the mind or spirit alone. It reflects the challenge to Cartesian dualism that the sociology of the body represents. From this perspective, as a result of being a body in contemporary society individuals face increasingly complex ethical decisions. Science, new technology and contemporary media provide more information on which to base these decisions but, at the same time, they produce new ethical dilemmas. It seems that ethics is forever playing 'catch up' with scientific developments (Giddens 1991; Beck 1992). This scenario of information overload and the multiplication of ethical issues has complicated rather than simplified ethical decision making, such that one can argue that morality has been personalized, privatized and problematized.

Contemporary life presents a situation in which it is no longer possible to look to 'tradition' or 'traditional authorities' for solutions to ethical dilemmas. Traditional bodies did not face such a prolif-eration of dilemmas (Bauman 1993, 1994). Moreover, contemporary life is marked by a decline in the certainty of religious, political and scientific authority (Shilling 1993). Indeed, such authorities both create and attempt to solve the ethical or moral problems of the late twentieth century. Our great-grandparents did not have to consider the pros and cons of reproduction without sexual intercourse nor did they have to make decisions concerning organ donation, much less consider the implications for humankind of the cloning of sheep or the genetic modification of food. They did not have to do so not merely because the technology behind these innovations did not exist. Technology, in its own time, is always new technology and, therefore, always more or less socially and morally problematic. Our great-grandparents did not have to consider these issues because some 'higher authority' would usually make so bold as to pronounce definitively on them. In short, they would have been made aware of the solutions rather than the problems produced by technological change. We, however, inhabit a society where those that seek to offer resolutions to moral or ethical dilemmas are implicated in their construction. Deference to a 'higher authority' in an age characterized by doubt about the efficacy of meta-narratives is problematic.

This proliferation and problematization of ethics is a sign of the times. Rasmussen (1990: 1) argues that our era is one in which ethics has become a cardinal signifier, to the extent 'that the Zeitgeist bears the mark of ethics'. This new 'spirit of the times' is further reinforced by a media discourse that speaks of a moral crisis, a society lacking in moral authority. UK Prime Minister Tony Blair's recent call for a new national moral agenda made good use of the recent moral panic surrounding the pregnant bodies of two 12-year-olds. They were pre-sented as symptoms of a society in need of a sense of order, a society that is struggling with new ethical dilemmas. This context encourages the emergence of a plurality of voices with new ethical claims. The moral agenda has changed rapidly over the past few decades, to the extent that we now inhabit a world that has become saturated with moral discourse.

We are 'aware', far more than our ancestors, of the social problems and moral issues of our times. We read and hear about, on a daily basis, social issues such as child abuse, violence towards women, homophobia, racism and environmental damage. It is not that these problems did not exist in the past. They did. Rather, broad social and cultural transformations, for example in the areas of gender inequality and environmental awareness, mean that these issues are at the fore-front of contemporary moral agendas. Our grandparents are unlikely to have examined their consciences over whether driving their cars to the bottle bank was better or worse for the environment than throwing the bottles in the rubbish bin in order to conserve petrol. In the 1950s the discovery of two pregnant 12-year-olds would not have featured in, never mind dominated for a couple of days, the national broadsheet and tabloid press. Nor would previous generations have considered 'Gazza's' participation in domestic violence as adequate grounds for his exclusion from the English football team. 'Wife beat-ing' would not have been considered as an issue worthy of excluding anybody from any public practice, because it would not have been a public concern. These ethical dilemmas would not have found a place on our ancestors' cultural agenda. The voices that might have put them there would not have been sufficiently influential.

McRobbie (1994b) points to the way in which 'marginalised groups' or 'their representatives' have become increasingly organized and vocal. They can now put their own ethical claims on to the moral agenda. The emergence of new social movements organized around 'issues' and identity politics has created a situation in which ethical bodies and their variable claims have become socially omnipresent. People who had previously been stamped with the mark of alterity such that their citizenship and moral status was in question – not for themselves but for the powers that be – have rebelled against this servitude and have, in the process, made the moral domain a contested site in which the very nature of truth and justice is contentious. Identity politics means the proliferation of carnal standpoints. Women, people of colour, and gay and disabled people point to a world that is not of their making and not to their liking. They cannot see themselves – other than in distorted form – in its moral mirror.

The good, the bad and the ugly

One outcome of the considerable expansion of our moral repertoire has been the development of an individual who, in the face of a plurality of beliefs, has acquired an outlook that is characterized by uncertainty and contingency (Vattimo 1992). The individual in 'late modernity' inhabits an increasingly uncertain and chaotic world in which self-identity is in permanent flux (Giddens 1991). The deconstruction of social certainty individualizes the questions of existence so that self-reflexivity becomes paramount. In 'high modernity' (Giddens 1991) people attempt to produce a sense of personal certainty through the construction of reflexive projects of self-identity. The search for 'ontological security' often takes a form such that everyday life is transformed into a series of reflexive somatically oriented projects which, taken together, constitute a quest for a unitary biography. For Giddens (1992: 31), the body features as 'a visible carrier of self-identity and is increasingly integrated into the lifestyle decisions which an individual makes'. Yet, there is a problem, even a paradox, because if both the world and the body are sites of ethical ambivalence, then they do not provide strong foundations for the construction of a secure and certain existence, let alone a reasonably consistent biographical narrative. Risk and anxiety are, therefore, the constant and unwelcome companions of projects of self-identity.

Giddens' (1991) argument contains connotations that seem to help to clarify the concept of identity and the place of ethics in contemporary society. It implies that identity construction is an active, fluid and diverse process. The self becomes a busy construction site and the body becomes defined by its flexibility in relation to the demands of rapidly changing cultural norms and values that are susceptible to the vacillations of fashion. These norms and values do not constrain reflexive projects of identity. On the contrary, they provide the resources or choices out of which identities are built. This connects the construction of self to the plurality of consumer goods and lifestyle options on offer in contemporary culture. One must note the centrality of consumer culture to the construction of identity. Yet, for Giddens (1991), consumer culture is not the site where ethics is constructed or experienced. His analysis does not allow for the different ways in which constraints, even in the arena of consumption, might prevent the reflexively orientated body from both constructing and pursuing its individually fashioned identity. Moreover, like Bauman (1993, 1996), Giddens argues that morality has been appropriated or sequestrated from the world of everyday experience by the increasing dominance, institutionalization and normalization of instrumental rationality. Thus, 'any reflexive project of the self, which carries so many possibilities for autonomy and happiness, has to be undertaken in the context of routines largely devoid of ethical content' (Giddens 1992: 176).

Giddens' (1992) emphasis on routines 'devoid of ethical content' in which individual projects of identity are developed would seem to fit well with the notion that consumer culture is hedonistic. Sense of self in consumer culture 'is profoundly connected with the idea of unlimited personal consumption', to such an extent that the dominant statement concerning self-identity in contemporary society has become 'I consume therefore I am'. The world is a supermarket, a space of infinite choice and minimal constraint (Giddens 1991, 1992). Normative regulation is reduced to the aesthetics of choice (taste) and the most important attribute that one requires should one wish to aspire to the 'good life ideal' in this moral desert is the ability to choose well (Bauman 1998: 31).

However, what is missing from this conception of the way in which consumer society works is recognition of the extent to which the consuming body embodies ethics. It thus fails to appreciate the potential that consumer culture contains for the development of an aesthetic ethic and a cultivated consumer (Falk 1994). This potential lies in the constraints imposed on the modern consuming self by the desire to seem cultivated. This constraint is especially visible in a world where aesthetics has been commodified such that value and beauty are translated into 'that which can be bought' (B.S. Turner 1994). Synnott's (1993) assertion that most purchases in the economy contain an aesthetic dimension exemplifies this point.

If reflexivity is central to the construction of identity in contemporary consumer culture, as Giddens (1991) argues, then it is not simply utilized to exercise choice. Instead, the commodification of the self through the consumption of 'desirable' goods, in order that they might bestow some of their magical qualities on us, reflects the contemporary consumer's concern with surface appearance and the 'stylization' of the body (Featherstone 1991b). To adapt a much-repeated aphorism, 'you are what you look like'. The beauty mystique boils down to two simple equations: beauty equals goodness and ugliness is equivalent to evil. As Synnott (1993: 78) notes, 'the morally good is physically beautiful and the evil is ugly'. Moreover, as Williams and Bendelow (1998b: 73) point out, this concern with surface appearance can be understood more accurately as an attempt on the part of the individual to control and construct – in the face of a plurality of values and lifestyle choices – the 'right kind of body'. This suggests that the ethic of the aesthetic, albeit in the moral desert of consumer culture, functions to regulate the body and its appearance. Nevertheless, the individual experiences aesthetic ethics as a form of constraint over consuming behaviour. This is due, to a large extent, to the way in which aesthetic discrimination, in an image-dominated society, is able to function as a powerful cultural norm (Featherstone 1991b). Synnott (1993: 101) testifies to the strength of this cultural norm. He writes: 'Aesthetic relations are perhaps as significant as class, gender or ethnic relations as determinants of life chances and aesthetic stratification as powerful as class, gender or ethnic stratification'. Goods are chosen carefully therefore, in order to signify, to both ourselves and others, who we desire to be.

The dialectic between aesthetics and ethics, the beautiful and the good, is not confined to contemporary consumer culture. The association between the beautiful and the moral (that is, between the beautiful and behavioural constraint) has a long history in European culture. A sense of the significance of this connection can be gained by taking a quick look at its conceptual career. Eagleton (1990: 13) draws attention to the way in which aesthetics, under the guidance of Baumgarten's eighteenth-century *Aesthetica*, arose as a 'discourse of the body'. Baumgarten's science of aesthetics was intended to refer to the sensational experience of the body. This science was also an attempt to bring the rather unruly bodily sensations associated with aesthetics under the control of the reflexive limits of reason. This effort culminated in Kant's attempt to define morality as an attribute of reason. However, Eagleton (1990) also notes that this form of aesthetic contemplation did not start with the Enlightenment. We have to journey back to the Greeks to witness the earliest interplay between beauty and virtue.

Synnott (1993) traces the origins of the beauty mystique to Socrates who, along with Plato, identified beauty with goodness at a metaphysical level. Aristotle's belief that beauty was God's gift was intensified in Christianity. Christianity's theology equated beauty and goodness with God. However, despite a somewhat ambivalent attitude towards mortal beauty, Christianity has, at various times, associated beauty with purity. The latter was regarded as a sign of being close to God or as a sign of the presence of God in the person. Popular culture has done much to solidify an aesthetic ethic (Synnott 1993). Examples abound. Renaissance beliefs held that physical beauty was an attribute of spiritual beauty. Romantic poets attempted to aestheticize the good. In Shakespearian drama, fairy tales (ancient and modern) and westerns the 'baddies' are always ugly. Synnott (1993: 95) concludes that beauty and ugliness, in contemporary society, feature not just as 'physical opposites' but also as 'moral opposites'.

Eagleton's (1990) monumental *The Ideology of the Aesthetic* traces the aesthetic-ethic connection right up to contemporary consumer culture. He describes the aestheticization of the everyday as a major feature of postwar society. The aesthetic elements of contemporary life are the major unifying force in a society where the efficacy of the 'real' is in decline. He argues that values have been aestheticized to such an extent that 'Morality is converted to a matter of style' (Eagleton 1990: 368). Eagleton as a Marxist is no lover of the postmodern so it is curious that his arguments are echoed by writers of a more postmodern temper, such as Mike Featherstone. Featherstone (1995: 44) also describes the 'tendency towards the aestheticisation of everyday life where life itself becomes the art project to be worked upon and constructed into a lifestyle'. For Featherstone (1995), this tendency has been propelled by two main factors. First, by movements and works in the art world such as Dada, the early Duchampian 'ready-mades' and the Surrealists, whose aim was to blur or dismantle the boundaries between art and everyday life. And second, by a 'hyper-real culture' – exemplified by Baudrillard and the film *Blade Runner* (released in 1982) – in which the image is everything, so that it is impossible to distinguish between appearance and reality. This twist to postmodern life is closely bound up with the tendency among certain contemporary theorists to use the body as the connective tissue that binds ethics to aesthetics. Featherstone (1995) cites the work of Foucault and Maffesoli as exemplary cases.

Foucault's (1997) conception of aesthetic ethics reveals itself in his discussion of the ways in which an individual body resists the monotonous regulation of the disciplinary powers of surveillance. He sought to explore the manner in which the subject's relationship with the self could be used to counter or resist the normalizing powers of modern society. By exploring this problem through an excursus on Greek ethics, Foucault at a stroke cuts the cord that was thought to exist between personal ethics and wider sociopolitical structures of morality. When asked, if there is no necessary relationship between ethics and other structures, then what kind of ethics is possible? he replies,

> What strikes me is the fact that in our society, art has become something which is related only to objects and not to individuals, or to life. That art is something which is specialized or which is done by experts who are artists. But couldn't everyone's life become a work of art? . . . From the idea that the self is not given to us, I think there is only one practical consequence: we have to create ourselves as a work of art.
>
> (Foucault 1997: 261–2)

In this excerpt, Foucault shows his debt to Nietzsche and his affinity with Baudelaire's 'dandy'. The emphasis is on individuals constructing themselves as ethical subjects. The individual has an obligation to make his or her lifestyle a thing of beauty. Virtuous existence – as it was for the Greeks – is accomplished by an exquisite life performance. The aesthetic attitude expressed by this conceptualization of aesthetic ethics is that of the detached, disinterested flâneur who strolls though life observing its banalities from a cool distance. It is elitist. For Foucault, ethics, as an art of existence, is a relationship one has with oneself. It is less a question of what 'it is right to do' and more a question of what 'it is right to be'.

Feeling bodies

Featherstone (1995) contrasts Foucault's individualistic conception of the aesthetic with Maffesoli's 'tribal' or collective orientation. There is another difference which is, perhaps, even more striking. Foucault's emphasis on the suave art of existence suggests that reason and self-control are still important players in the performance of any ethical drama. Maffesoli (1996) grounds ethics in the passionate processes of group solidarity. In other words, Maffesoli stresses the Dionysian legacy of Nietzsche, whereas Foucault still finds some virtue in the temperate Apollonian element of the German philosopher's work (Eagleton 1990; B.S. Turner 1994). Therefore, whereas Foucault describes the 'ethical subject' as the embodiment of the rational beautiful self, Maffesoli founds ethics on 'puissance' – the vitality and emotional energy that arises in and through people's everyday 'tribal' affiliations. It is not the body but bodies, or more precisely 'the emotional community', that are the 'home' of ethical experience. Maffesoli distinguishes his aesthetic ethic from the thinkers reviewed in the previous section by grounding it not in the rationalist tradition of personal development, but in an interesting mix of vitalism and collectivism in which the affects loom large.

Maffesoli (1996: 9) refers to the privileging of the individual as 'the problem of individualism', a misconception that, he argues, obscures the development of contemporary sociality. For Maffesoli (1996: 16), then, the focus is on the inter-corporeal multiplicity of formal groups and temporary groupings that enliven our daily existence. These, he argues, are central to and the embodiment of our experience of life. These groups are made up of those who think and feel as we do, not on a rational but on an emotional and aesthetic level. Ethics arises out of the emotional relations, out of the 'shared feeling' of 'tribal' affiliation and participation. Maffesoli (1996: 20) argues that 'the collective sensibility which issues from the aesthetic form results in an ethical connection'. The ethic is 'the glue that holds together the diverse elements of a given whole'. The groups therefore represent, however fleetingly, an aesthetic community, a collective rather than an individual expression of 'the ethics of the aesthetic' (Featherstone 1995: 47).

Furthermore, ethics as embodied experience is much more evident in Maffesoli's work than in Foucault's. Foucault emphasizes the importance of 'critical self reflection' in the living of the aesthetic life (Eagleton 1990: 393). This produces an individual concerned, singularly, with technique and appearance. There is no sign of a properly embodied conception of ethics in Foucault's account of the aesthetic, because there is no sign of 'the tabooed realms of affection, emotional intimacy and compassion'. These 'tabooed realms' do, however, feature strongly in Maffesoli's (1996) analysis where the aesthetic ethic is characterized by sensuality and relationships in which the affects are very much to the fore. It is empathy rather than reason that sustains the bonds of an 'emotional community'. Accordingly, Maffesoli (1996: 11) distinguishes between the contractually based relations of goal orientated rational subjects and the 'empathetic sociality' and sensuality of group relations 'which is expressed by a succession of ambiences, feelings and emotions'. Yet, as Bauman (1993: 143) points out as part of his project to separate out the ethical and the aesthetic, the sociality of 'neo-tribes' is too ephemeral to constitute a proper basis for moral action.

Bauman (1993, 1994, 1995, 1996) does not place the frisson of collective relations at the heart of his 'redemptive critique of morality'

(Delanty 1999: 100). On the contrary, ethics – after the collapse of religion and the ethical rule of law that externalized ethical decision making – is embodied in the loneliness of the postmodern moral actor who lives, uneasily, with the ambivalence of ethical choice. Bauman (1993: 11) argues that 'moral phenomena are inherently "non-rational" ' because moral responsibility (or responsibility for the other) precedes rational calculation. The rationalization of ethics in modernity 'substitutes the learnable knowledge of rules for the moral self constituted by responsibility'. The moral context is ambivalent and 'aporetic', that is contradictory, and the moral self is radically uncertain, 'feeling' its way through the vicissitudes of moral action. However, Bauman's postmodern 'ethics of responsibility' does not envisage a special place for embodiment. But this neglect evaporates when he discusses the philosophy of Emmanuel Levinas. Levinas (1981) argues that 'ethics' is 'first philosophy' because it inhabits a 'pre-ontological' space in which there is no limit to responsibility. Levinas is at the centre of a search for moral creativity that grounds virtue in a non-reciprocal, asymmetrical and sensual sense of responsibility for the other. This can be summarized by the claim that postmodern ethics must be understood as an 'ethics of caress' (Ouakinin, quoted in Bauman 1993: 92).

Ethics in modernity has been constituted not only in a rationalist frame of reference but also by the assumption that 'to see is to know'. Martin Jay (1994) calls this 'ocularcentrism'. Modernity is a visual culture derived from Cartesian perspectivalism, but cultural critique in the twentieth century has increasingly become a critique of the 'assertoric' nature of the gaze. The 'assertoric' gaze is hard, intransigent, objectifying, inflexible and exclusionary. Its paradigm is scientific observation and dispassionate reason and it demands distance and disinterestedness (Levin 1988). It underpins the way in which we make sense of and labour in our modern world and so it has a profound influence on the values that promote ethical thought and action.

Even though the postmodern turn implies a world of hyper-visuality and a proliferation of images shorn of their referents, there is in postmodern times a 'powerful antiocular impulse' which is best represented in the work of Levinas and Luce Irigaray (Jay 1994: 546). It is possible to claim that there is an 'aletheic' gaze, which is an open, caring, flexible and inclusionary gaze (Levin 1988). But even this meaning may not embody sufficient value to cradle a revaluing of ethical values, because the visual is too profoundly implicated in phallocentric culture: 'More than any other sense, the eye objectifies and masters' (Irigaray, quoted in Classen 1997: 50). The gaze is dominated by its masculine, 'assertoric' meaning such that it constitutes women as passive objects of contemplation. Ethics, therefore, must appropriate another sense, and touch – the most primordial of all the senses despite its strong association with power, abuse and violence – is the most likely candidate. In an essay entitled 'The fecundity of the caress', Irigaray (1993: 186) – with Levinas as interlocutor – writes that touch 'binds and unbinds two others in a flesh that is still and always untouched by mastery'. Elsewhere (Irigaray 1985: 144), she argued that the 'style' of women prioritizes proximity over distance and therefore 'does not privilege sight: instead, it takes each figure back to its source, which is among other things *tactile*'. Although touch is 'ranked low on the sensorium', it is 'of first importance for our physical health, our emotional life and our intellectual development' (Synnott 1993: 156–7). Increasingly, it is also being celebrated as a bearer of moral development.

The reinvention of ethics embodied in the claims made by Irigaray and Bauman have their roots in the anti-ontological project of Emmanuel Levinas. To get to ethics one has to forgo or get behind or beyond the philosophical preoccupation with 'being' that is central to logocentric and ocularcentric thought. For Levinas, 'Ethical obligation arises not from the logical and ontological universality of reason . . . but rather immediately from the uniqueness of the moral situation itself' (Ciaramelli 1991: 85). We can avoid the complex arguments that take the reader of Levinas 'beyond being' and propose that it is the immediacy and proximity of the other that, in itself, makes a claim of responsibility on 'me' that I cannot resist. To be 'face to face' with the other is to be in the realm of intimacy and morality. To caress without reciprocation or condition – the epitome of motherly love – is to enter the realm of the moral self – that is, the self which is *for* the other. Love, touch, morality, the body and, finally, for both Levinas and Bauman (1995), community are the key players in the making of moral citizens, and yet these are all categories and conditions that thrive on ambivalence and have been, in modernity, desiccated and rationalized. In the contemporary world, the possibility for ethical success and ethical failure remains more open than it has ever been.

Conclusion

To explore the way in which the body embodies or lives ethics lands us in the lap of philosophy and social theory. This is the position from which the potential of the sociology of the body is being developed. Discontents with modernity have inspired parallel debate about ethics and the body. It seems that the lines are now on a course of convergence and as ethics struggles with its logocentric inheritance, the body as the seat of desire becomes an obvious channel in which ethical discourse can relaunch itself. If 'moral phenomena are inherently non-rational' (Bauman 1993: 11), then it is hardly surprising that contemporary ethical debate is establishing its discourse in and alongside the ethical realm and in the ambivalent and sensual domains of feeling and touch. If ambiguity and uncertainty are the constant companions of ethical choice, then the effort to base ethics on rational-legal authority is fruitless and the ethical self is likely to live, if anywhere, inside the skin of an 'intimate' community. The notion of community, however, is also ambivalent and problematic. If it is (neo)tribal, it is too ephemeral to provide an adequate context for embodied ethics. It needs to be open and tolerant, to be able to respect identity and to maintain and transcend differences. This may be possible but it is doubtful that many would bet on it. Yet, despite the ambivalent nature of the contemporary social context and the popularity of the none too persuasive argument that postmodernity and consumer culture spell the end of ethics, the body has increasingly come to be conceptualized as the major site of ethical identity. Indeed, even if the body is conceptualized only at the level of representation or symbol, ethics is still a necessary focus. Even in its stunted form as an embodied 'art of existence', ethics can tell a story about what counts as 'value' in contemporary society.

However, there is more to the story, more to ethics than its (potentially dangerous) accommodation to the superficial sensibilities of fashion and appearance. Where feelings rather than image emerge as the dominant theme in contemporary debates about moral action, then the potential for a sociology of embodied ethics – exemplified in the work of Zygmunt Bauman – manifests itself. Levinas (1981) is clearly the philosophical master of this development and his call for embodied ethics as an ethics of responsibility has had a powerful impact on the work of Bauman (1993) and Irigaray (1993). It is the stress on the emotional rather than the rational that goes a long way towards providing a fuller and more embodied account of the ethical body. If the ethical body is to transcend the limits of reflexive projects of self, then Levinas' ethical conception of alterity, in which the other is ethically prior to 'me', is a basis on which to develop further an (ethical?) sociology of embodied ethics.

Further reading

Terry Eagleton's (1990) introductory chapter to *The Ideology of the Aesthetic* (entitled 'Free Particulars') offers a detailed account of the way in which aesthetics originated as a philosophy of the body. It also offers a potted account of Platonic, Kantian, Hegelian and phenomenological approaches to aesthetics and morality that are perhaps more accessible to those interested in the sociology of the body than the more detailed chapters in the rest of the text. In a similar way Bryan Turner's (1994) introduction to Buci-Glucksmann's (1994) *Baroque Reason: The Aesthetics of Modernity* traces aesthetics in relation to the development of social theory. Although Turner's primary concern, given the focus of Buci-Glucksmann's work, is Walter Benjamin, he still offers a good general account of the connections between aesthetics and 'the good'. The style of Emmanuel Levinas' writing can be rather difficult for the uninitiated. There are, however, plenty of introductions, interviews and commentaries that serve to orient those who are new to his work. Levinas' general philosophy is perhaps most accessible in the excellent interviews conducted by Richard Kearney in Cohen's (1986) *Face to Face with Levinas*. Sean Hand's (1989) *The Levinas Reader* offers many of the philosopher's original and most important essays. The commentaries that accompany it are clear and concise. Martin Jay's (1994) discussion of Levinas in 'The ethics of blindness and the postmodern sublime: Levinas and Lyotard', which is part of his massive *Downcast Eyes: The Denigration of Vision in Twentieth-Century French Thought*, is a convincing and accomplished account of Levinas' influence on the development of postmodern theory. Jay does this primarily by way of a discussion of Levinas' emphasis on proximity and touch, and highlights the influence this has had on feminist ethics. The most accessible guide to the ways in which 'corporeal feminists' have tackled embodied ethics, Margrit Shildrick's (1997) *Leaky Bodies and Boundaries*, is the best bet. Last but not least, one must read Zygmunt Bauman. He is a prolific writer who writes extensively about ethics. Of all his works on the topic, if I had to choose one, it would be *Postmodern Ethics* (1993).

Conclusion

Whether a book such as this requires a conclusion is questionable. Within each chapter 'key' points have been re-emphasized, recurring themes have been summarized and questions for further consideration have been raised. As such, to go over the same ground once again may seem to be simply a waste of time and effort, particularly for the reader, who is likely to gain little in the way of new information or refined insight into the material previously covered.

However, this collection has not only raised questions and explored themes specific to the subject matter of each individual chapter; it has also engaged with what, for many readers, can be understood as a series of ideas, propositions and problematics that in many ways suggest a far broader historical shift in our understanding of the relationship between the body and the cultural sensibility that dominates contemporary westernized societies. As we suggested in our 'Introduction', and then emphasized in several of the subsequent chapters, the evidence of a growing fascination with the body among sociologists should not be seen as an isolated phenomenon. As Bill Hughes stressed in his discussion of 'Medicalized bodies' in Chapter 1, as the ways in which we think about the nature of reality have changed and the limits of previous technologies have been superseded, both science and philosophy have started to reconceptualize the body. Indeed, while it may be a little too easy to reduce the body to a metaphor that encapsulates the paradoxes of the contemporary cultural and scientific spirit, the temptation to do so is extremely attractive. For, in many respects, the body has emerged as *the* signifier of the so-called postmodern age. Its association with the libidinal or Dionysian dimension of life has set it up in opposition to the Enlightenment belief in progress through reason that posited the sublimation of the carnal in the cognitive. Meanwhile, as Elizabeth Jagger argues in Chapter 3, the body is paramount in the images and values associated with consumerism, suggesting its complicity in the propagation and indeed celebration of the superficiality of contemporary consumer culture – themes that sit at the heart of the postmodern condition.

Believe it or not?

Of course, it is easy from our relatively privileged position to make such sweeping assertions about the body as a topic of serious academic scrutiny. What we are more concerned with, however, is how you, the reader, have responded to the ideas and arguments developed in this book. Having read some, or perhaps even all of it, hopefully you will now feel rather more familiar, and even possibly comfortable, with the proposition that the human body is something that sociological analysis can illuminate. For, although the idea that the body can be conceptualized as a social or cultural category became – in modernity – an almost counterintuitive one, this process is now somewhat in reverse, and we suspect that those readers who have approached this volume with a healthy scepticism about the discourse of the 'natural body' will be those who have benefited most. If this is not the case, however, and you are still bound to a form of corporeal naturalism, then your incredulity has probably a lot to do with the palpable, material experience of living life as, and in, a body. The body as something apparently created in a pre-social environment leads you to resist what you see as a largely misguided attempt by sociologists to dabble in matters that are clearly outside their sphere of competence. Alternatively, you might be concerned that any undue emphasis on the corporeal dimension of human life may result in an unnecessary marginalization of the mind and the intellectual dimension of being; one that runs the risk of turning into a form of naive romanticism at best or, at worst, a full-blooded nihilism.

If the latter is the case, we have to say that we would not necessarily look on it as a sign of failure in what we have attempted to do here. To nurture doubt and the faculty of criticism is as much a part of the sociological project as is the handing down of 'correct facts' or 'applicable theories'. However, if we take a moment to reflect on such objections, we may see that they serve more to support our endeavours than to undermine them. For being able to disagree about the status of this thing called the body suggests that the concept is indeed a contestable one; that the ways in which we think and talk about our own and other people's bodies, and the ways in which we classify, order and manipulate bodies, are not natural or immutable practices but essentially socially defined acts. Such acts are not, therefore, based *solely* on individual whims and fancies or on the dictates of nature, but on culturally located and socially significant ideas and practices. In their discussion of 'Disabled bodies' (Chapter 2), for example, Kevin Paterson and Bill Hughes emphasized that recent sociological debates on disability have begun to problematize 'a disembodied view of disability', one that fails to develop an adequate sociology of impairment, a phenomenon that it designates as a pre-social given. In many respects, as we emphasized in our 'Introduction', the classical sociological claim that the body belongs to biologists seems to have collapsed and with this collapse the meaning of the body has become a 'problem' for linguistic, cultural and social analysis as well as biology. Indeed, what makes the body such a fascinating object for sociologists is the way in which its study serves to problematize the distinction between the biological and the sociological, the natural and the cultural.

I ain't got (no)body

Yet despite making such grand claims about the sociology of the body as the signifier of a new cultural sensibility, even as we write we are aware that we may well be standing on the brink of an age in which the everyday significance of the human body may be in decline. As Lyotard (1991: 13) has suggested, the question that will face humankind in the future is that of 'how to make thought without a body possible?' – a question based on the proposition that the body will come to be increasingly viewed as a liability, and as such will be superseded by the computer as the depository of thought and creativity. Indeed, we can already observe how the development of new technologies of communication and entertainment, particularly those associated with computer-generated realities, and the emergence of cyberspace as a domain of human interaction, have cast doubt as to the necessity of the material body to our everyday lives. It could be argued that in cyberspace, for example, we can leave the limitations of our physical bodies behind. Our appearance, biological sex and our physical abilities are all there to be invented and reinvented, where imagination is the only limit. Certainly, computer games have already made world-class winners, in a range of 'sports', out of individuals whose physical skills had, perhaps until recently, debarred them from success in the 'embodied' versions of such competitions. Advances in medical technology – the ability to replace essential organs such as the heart or lungs with mechanical devices, for instance – although far from perfected, hint at a future in which the body ceases to be a limitation, and in which the futuristic idea of the cyborg becomes an everyday reality. Indeed, perhaps our future is best captured in the even more extreme image, beloved of so many popular science-fiction writers, of the disembodied cerebrum, sustained by technology and linked to its own reality through implants and computer-generated images.

It would, however, in our view at least, be a mistake to confuse such developments with the immanent 'death of the body'. Rather, in many respects, what such developments indicate is an intensification of the relationship between the body and society, and, as such, an increase in its significance for sociology in particular. The ability to redefine our physicality in cyberspace cannot be separated from the sociocultural expectations we may take with us on our virtual journey, impacting, for example, on how we perceive our bodies and, in doing so, may redefine the nature of inter-corporeality and inter-subjectivity. It also raises important questions, particularly for sociologists, about the potential impact such technologies might have on the very nature of social relations. If, as Rachel Russell has suggested in Chapter 6, ethical behaviour is premised on embodied interaction, what challenge does this virtual world pose for traditional modes of social solidarity, and even for our sense of right and wrong or good and evil?

Equally, improvements in our ability to substitute bodily parts with manufactured devices pose a range of ethical questions, such as who should have access to these biotechnologies, and at what point does society cease to ascribe the status of humanity to a body that is part artificial implant? As the complexity of social tasks increases, and we become more and more dependent on the technologies around us, to what extent do they impact on the shape and meaning of our bodies? For example, as this conclusion is typed, we may want to consider the question of, 'where does the body end and the computer we are using begin?' As daily computer users, our bodily skills and reflexes are as much the product of the design of the computer keyboard and the angle of the monitor as they are of either intentional activity or the physical structure of our bodies. In turn, this raises the question of 'who decided to design the computer in this manner, and why did they do so?' We suspect that factors such as the size of the keyboard, the dimension of the screen and the angle at which the monitor is viewed have as much to do with a socially organized conception of fashion, for example, as they have with any 'rational' principle of ergonomic design and, as such, they have significant implications for the relationship between bodily comportment and cultural expectation.

It may be, therefore, that it is more than a little premature to talk of the demise of the body, either as an integral dimension of what it is to be human, or equally, as a vital subject of concern for sociologists. As Philip Hancock and Melissa Tyler stressed in their exploration of 'Working bodies' in Chapter 5, the very fact that technologies, both material and social, are increasingly central to how we use and conceptualize our bodies suggests quite the contrary. Now, more than ever it seems, sociologists should be sensitive to the impact of embodied practices on a whole host of socially determined beliefs and practices.

Beyond the duality of mind and body

Having attempted to make a case for the continuing, if not increasing, relevance of the body for contemporary sociological inquiry, it is perhaps also important to reflect on some of the potential pitfalls of an overzealous identification with the corporeal. For, lest we should forget, as a number of the authors here have pointed out, the re-emergence of the body in sociological thought was as much a reaction to the consequences of an Enlightenment-inspired fascination with the realm of the mind as it was a direct acknowledgement of the body itself. As such, the sociology of the body has sought to redress what has come to be perceived as an imbalance; a dualism that has tended to denigrate the corporeal dimension of human life in favour of the intellectual and cognitive basis of human understanding. However, in reversing this prioritization of the cognitive, the danger is that all we may succeed in doing is establishing new hierarchies, and produce new modes of forgetting that subsume the previously dominant term under its newly valorized 'Other'.

If we do not take care then, it may be that the status of mind as an integral dimension of human being could itself be forgotten in our rush to embrace the body as the source of all insight into, and explanation of, the complexities of contemporary social life. Such an error would not only, in philosophical terms, demonstrate a profound lack of ontological judgement but would also undermine the ability of sociology to engage with the richness and complexity of what it is to 'be' a corporeal-intellectual being. Nor must we let our considerations end at the physical limits of the human body. As we noted previously, our bodies are themselves intimately entwined, on a daily basis, with material objects that, at one and the same time, enable, disable, as-cribe value to and denigrate the corporeal. Very often our bodies have meanings for others and ourselves only when they occupy particular spaces and locations or move through specific temporal contexts – a point implicit in Emmanuelle Tulle-Winton's discussion of the socio-cultural context of 'Old bodies' in Chapter 4. As Rose (1996: 143) has so eloquently emphasized, 'human being is dispersed. It is emplaced, enacted through a regime of devices, gazes, techniques that extend beyond the limits of the flesh and into spaces, assemblages'. As such, approaches represented by the likes of Actor Network Theory (see Law and Hassard 1999) which seek to deconstruct not only the dualism of mind and body but that of human and non-human, may be of use to us in our future attempts to develop our understanding of the place of the body within society.

Whatever direction the sociology of the body develops in the future, one thing would seem to be certain, however. A concern with the body has now been firmly (re)established in a range of vital areas of soci-ological inquiry and research, and is unlikely to find itself so easily marginalized again. As such, we hope that this book will provide a valuable jumping-off point, encouraging you to look beyond the material contained here and to reconsider the relationship between the sociocultural and the corporeal. As we tried to stress in our 'Introduction', our treatment of the body in this book was never intended to be exhaustive. Rather its objective was very much to offer you a taste of the current sociological interest in the body. As such, it sought merely to whet the appetites of its readers, and to encourage experimentation with a more diverse range of ideas and material than that currently on offer. After all, sociology is, by its very nature, a dynamic discipline – one embedded in a world that is constantly undergoing change and upheaval. As our relationships to this thing we call 'the body', and between the individual and society, develop and change, so sociology needs to be at the forefront of mapping out and trying to come to terms with such changes. Perhaps, then, the most interesting questions are those yet to be asked, and the most difficult challenges to our understanding are those yet to be faced.

References

Abberley, P. (1987) The concept of oppression and the development of a social theory of disability, *Disability, Handicap and Society*, 2(1): 5–19.

Abberley, P. (1997) The limits of classical social theory in the analysis and transformation of disablement (Can this really be the end; to be stuck inside of Mobile with the Memphis Blues again?), in L. Barton and M. Oliver (eds) *Disability Studies: Past, Present and Future*. Leeds: The Disability Press.

Abberley, P. (1999) Book reviews, *Disability and Society*, 14(5): 693–7.

Adkins, L. (1995) *Gendered Work*. Milton Keynes: Open University Press.

Alt, J. (1976) Beyond class: The decline of labour and leisure, *Telos*, 28: 22–43.

Amin, A. (1994) Post-Fordism: Models, fantasies and phantoms of transition, in A. Amin (ed.) *Post-Fordism: A Reader*. Oxford: Blackwell.

Arber, S. and Ginn, J. (eds) (1995) *Connecting Gender and Ageing: A Sociological Approach*. Buckingham: Open University Press.

Armstrong, D. (1987) Theoretical tensions in biopsychosocial medicine, *Social Science and Medicine*, 25(11): 183–91.

Armstrong, D. (1993) From clinical gaze to a regime of total health, in A. Beattie, M. Gott, L. Jones and M. Sidell (eds) *Health and Wellbeing: A Reader*. London: Macmillan.

Armstrong, D. (1994) Bodies of knowledge/knowledge of bodies, in C. Jones and R. Porter (eds) *Re-assessing Foucault: Power, Medicine and the Body*. London: Routledge.

Ashton, J. and Seymour, H. (1988) *The New Public Health*. Milton Keynes: Open University Press.

Atkinson, P. (1988) Description and diagnosis: Reproducing normal medicine, in M. Lock and D. Gordon (eds) *Biomedicine Examined*. London: Kluwer.

Austoker, J. and Evans, J. (1992) Breast self-examination, in T. Heller, L. Bailey and S. Pattison (eds) *Preventing Cancers*. Milton Keynes: Open University Press.

Barnes, C. (1994) *Disabled People in Britain and Discrimination*. London: Hirst & Company.

Barnes, C. (1998) The social model of disability: A sociological phenomenon ignored by sociologists, in T. Shakespeare (ed.) *The Disability Reader: Social Science Perspectives*. London: Cassell.

Barnes, C. and Mercer, G. (eds) (1996) *Exploring the Divide: Illness and Disability*. Leeds: The Disability Press.

Barnes, C. and Mercer, G. (eds) (1997) *Doing Disability Research*. Leeds: The Disability Press.

Barnes, C., Mercer, G. and Shakespeare, T. (1999) *Exploring Disability: A Sociological Introduction*. Cambridge: Polity.

Barry, D. and Hazen, M.A. (1996) Do you take your body to work?, in D. Boje, R. Gephart Jr and T. Thatchenkey (eds) *Postmodern Management and Organization Theory*. London: Sage.

Bartky, S.L. (1990) *Femininity and Domination*. London: Routledge.

Barton, L. (ed.) (1996) *Disability and Society: Emerging Issues and Insights*. Harlow: Longman.

Barton, L. (1997) Sociology and disability: Some emerging issues, in L. Barton and M. Oliver (eds) *Disability Studies: Past, Present and Future*. Leeds: The Disability Press.

Barton, L. and Oliver, M. (eds) (1997) *Disability Studies: Past, Present and Future*. Leeds: The Disability Press.

Baudrillard, J. (1975) *The Mirror of Production*. St Louis: Teleos Press.

Baudrillard, J. (1983) *Simulations*. New York: Semiotext(e).

Baudrillard, J. (1988a) *America*. London: Verso.

Baudrillard, J. (1988b) *Selected Writings*. Cambridge: Polity Press.

Bauman, Z. (1987) *Legislators and Interpreters. On Modernity, Postmodernity and Intellectuals*. Cambridge: Polity Press.

Bauman, Z. (1991) *Modernity and Ambivalence*. Cambridge: Polity Press.

Bauman, Z. (1993) *Postmodern Ethics*. Oxford: Blackwell.

Bauman, Z. (1994) *Alone Again: Ethics after Certainty*. London: Demos.

Bauman, Z. (1995) *Life in Fragments: Essays in Postmodern Morality*. Oxford: Blackwell.

Bauman, Z. (1996) Morality in the age of contingency, in P. Heelas, S. Lash and P. Morris (eds) *Detraditionalization*. Cambridge: Polity Press.

Bauman, Z. (1998) *Work, Consumerism and the New Poor*. Buckingham: Open University Press.

Beck, U. (1992) *Risk Society: Towards a New Modernity*. London: Sage.

Bell, D. (1976) *The Cultural Contradictions of Capitalism*. London: Heinemann.

Bendelow, G. and Williams, S. (1995) Transcending the dualisms: Towards a sociology of pain, *Sociology of Health and Illness*, 17: 139–65.

Benson, S. (1997) The body, health and eating disorders, in K. Woodward (ed.) *Identity and Difference*. London: Sage, in association with The Open University.

Bentham, J. (1995) *The Panopticon Writings*. London: Verso (first published 1791).

Biggs, S. (1997) Choosing not to be old? Masks, bodies and identity management in later life, *Ageing and Society*, 17: 553–70.

Biggs, S. (1999) *The Mature Imagination: Dynamics of Identity in Midlife and Beyond*. Buckingham: Open University Press.

Birren, J.E. and Bengtson, V.L. (1988) *Emergent Theories of Aging*. New York: Springer.

Blaikie, A. and Hepworth, M. (1997) Representations of old age in painting and photography, in A. Jamieson, S. Harper and C.R. Victor (eds) *Critical Approaches to Ageing and Later Life*. Buckingham: Open University Press.

Bocock, R. (1993) *Consumption*. London: Routledge.

Boje, D. (1995) Stories of the storytelling organization: A postmodern analysis of Disney as Tamara-Land, *Academy of Management Journal*, 38(4): 997–1035.

Bordo, S. (1993) *Unbearable Weight: Feminism, Western Culture, and the Body*. Berkeley, CA: University of California Press.

Bourdieu, P. (1984) *Distinction: A Social Critique of the Judgement of Taste*. Cambridge, MA: Harvard University Press.

Braverman, H. (1974) *Labor and Monopoly Capital*. New York: Monthly Review Press.

Brewis, J. (1998) What is wrong with this picture? Sex and gender relations in *Disclosure*, in J. Hassard and R. Holliday (eds) *Organization Representation*. London: Sage.

Bronner, S.J. (ed.) (1989) *Consuming Visions: Accumulation and Display of Goods in America 1880–1920*. New York: W.W. Norton.

Bunton, R. and Burrows, R. (1995) Consumption and health in the epidemiological clinic of late modern medicine, in R. Bunton, S. Nettleton and R. Burrows (eds) *The Sociology of Health Promotion*. London: Routledge.

Bunton, R., Nettleton, S. and Burrows, R. (eds) (1995) *The Sociology of Health Promotion*. London: Routledge.

Burrell, G. (1984) Sex and organizational analysis, *Organization Studies*, 5(2): 97–118.

Burrell, G. (1988) Modernism, postmodernism and organizational analysis: The contribution of Michel Foucault, *Organization Studies*, 9(2): 221–35.

Burrell, G. (1997) *Pandemonium: Towards a Retro-Organization Theory*. London: Sage.

Bury, M. (1982) Chronic illness as biographical disruption, *Sociology of Health and Illness*, 4(2): 167–92.

Bury, M. (1995) Ageing, gender and sociological theory, in S. Arber and J. Ginn (eds) *Connecting Gender and Ageing: A Sociological Approach*. Buckingham: Open University Press.

Bury, M. (1996) Defining and researching disability: Challenges and responses, in C. Barnes and G. Mercer (eds) *Exploring the Divide: Illness and Disability*. Leeds: The Disability Press.

Bury, M. (1997) *Health and Illness in a Changing Society*. London: Routledge.

Butler, J. (1989) *Gender Trouble. Feminism and the Subversion of Identity*. London: Routledge.

Butler, J. (1993) *Bodies That Matter; on the Discursive Limits of 'Sex'*. London: Routledge.

Bytheway, B. (1993) Ageing and biography: The letters of Bernard and Mary Berenson, *Sociology*, 27(1): 153–65.

Bytheway, B. and Johnson, J. (1998) The sight of age, in S. Nettleton and J. Watson (eds) *The Body in Everyday Life*. London: Routledge.

Campbell, J. and Oliver, M. (1996) *Disability Politics: Understanding our Past, Changing our Future*. London: Routledge.

Canguilhem, G. (1998) *The Normal and the Pathological*. New York: Zone Books (trans. C.R. Fawcett and R.S. Cohen).

Chaney, D. (1983) The department store as a cultural form, *Theory, Culture and Society* 1(3): 22–31.

Chaney, D. (1996) *Lifestyles*. London: Routledge.

Charmaz (1983) Loss of self: A fundamental form of suffering in the chronically ill, *Sociology of Health and Illness*, 5: 168–95.

Ciaramelli, F. (1991) Levinas's ethical discourse: Between individuation and universality, in R. Bernasconi and S. Critchley (eds) *Re-Reading Levinas*. Bloomington, IN: Indiana University Press.

Cixous, H. (1994) Sonia Rykiel in translation, in S. Benstock and S. Ferriss (eds) *On Fashion*. New Brunswick, NJ: Rutgers University Press.

Clark, H., Chandler, J. and Barry, J. (eds) (1994) *Organizations and Identities*. London: Chapman and Hall.

Classen, C. (1997) Engendering perception: Gender ideologies and sensory hierarchies in western history, *Body and Society*, 1: 43–63.

Cockburn, C. (1991) *In the Way of Women*. London: Macmillan.

Cohen, R.A. (1986) *Face to Face with Levinas*. Albany, NY: State University of New York Press.

Cole, T.R. (1997) *The Journey of Life: A Cultural History of Aging in America*. Cambridge: Cambridge University Press.

Cooper, N., Stevenson, C. and Hale, G. (1996) *Integrating Perspectives on Health*. Buckingham: Open University Press.

Corker, M. (1999) Differences, conflations and foundations: The limits to 'accurate' theoretical representation of disabled people's experience, *Disability and Society*, 14(5): 627–42.

Corker, M. and French, S. (eds) (1999) *Disability Discourse*. Buckingham: Open University Press.

Corrigan, P. (1996) *The Sociology of Consumption*. London: Sage.

Cross, G. (1993) *Time and Money: The Making of Consumer Culture*. London: Routledge.

Crossley, N. (1995) Merleau-Ponty, the elusive body and carnal sociology, *Body and Society*, 1(1): 43–63.

Crow, L. (1996) Including all of our lives: Renewing the social model of disability, in J. Morris (ed.) *Encounters with Strangers: Feminism and Disability*. London: The Women's Press.

Csordas, T. (1993) Somatic modes of attention, *Cultural Anthropology*, 8(2): 135–56.

Csordas, T. (1994) *Embodiment and Experience: The Existential Ground of Culture and Self*. Cambridge: Cambridge University Press.

Cumming, D. (1996) *Pretty Ribbons*. Zurich: Stemmle AG.

Cunningham-Burley, S. and Backett-Milburn, K. (1998) The body, health and self in the middle years, in S. Nettleton and J. Watson (eds) *The Body in Everyday Life*. London: Routledge.

Dale, K. (2000) *Under the Knife*. London: Macmillan.

Davis, K. (1993) On the movement, in J. Swain, V. Finkelstein, S. French and M. Oliver (eds) *Disabling Barriers – Enabling Environments*. London: Sage.

Davis, K. (1995) *Reshaping the Female Body: The Dilemma of Cosmetic Surgery*. London: Routledge.

Davis, K. (ed.) (1997a) *Embodied Practices: Feminist Perspectives on the Body*. London: Sage.

Davis, K. (1997b) My body is my art: Cosmetic surgery as feminist utopia, in K. Davis (ed.) *Embodied Practices: Feminist Perspectives on the Body*. London: Sage.

Davis, L. (1995) *Enforcing Normalcy: Disability, Deafness and the Body*. London and New York: Verso.

Davis, L. (ed.) (1997) *The Disability Studies Reader*. New York and London: Routledge.

De Beauvoir, S. (1970) *La Vieillesse*. Paris: Gallimard.

Delanty, G. (1997) *Social Science: Beyond Constructivism and Realism*. Buckingham: Open University Press.

Delanty, G. (1999) *Social Theory in a Changing World*. Cambridge: Polity Press.

Department of Health (1991) *The Patient's Charter*. London: HMSO.

Diprose, R. (1994) *The Bodies of Women: Ethics, Embodiment and Sexual Difference.* London: Routledge.

Dubos, R. (1960) *Mirage of Health. Utopias: Progress and Biological Change.* London: George Allen and Unwin.

Durkheim, E. (1984) *The Division of Labour in Society.* London: Macmillan (first published 1893).

Dyer, G. (1982) *Advertising as Communication.* London: Methuen.

Eagleton, T. (1990) *The Ideology of the Aesthetic.* Oxford: Blackwell.

Elias, N. (1978) *The History of Manners: The Civilizing Process, Volume One.* Oxford: Blackwell.

Elshtian, J.B. and Cloyd, T.C. (1995) *Politics and the Human Body: Assault on Dignity.* Nashville, TN: Vanderbilt University Press.

Engel, G. (1977) The need for a new medical model: A challenge for biomedicine, *Science,* 196(129): 164–71.

Estes, C.L. (1979) *The Aging Experience.* San Francisco, CA: Jossey Bass.

Evans, C. and Thornton, M. (1989) *Women and Fashion.* London: Quartet.

Ewen, S. (1976) *Captains of Consciousness: Advertising and the Social Roots of the Consumer Culture.* New York: McGraw-Hill.

Ewen, S. and Ewen, E. (1982) *Channels of Desire.* New York: McGraw-Hill.

Fairhurst, E. (1998) 'Growing old gracefully' as opposed to 'mutton dressed as lamb': The social construction of recognising older women, in S. Nettleton and J. Watson (eds) *The Body in Everyday Life.* London: Routledge.

Falk, P. (1994) *The Consuming Body.* London: Sage.

Featherstone, M. (1991a) The body in consumer culture, in M. Featherstone, M. Hepworth and B.S. Turner (eds) *The Body: Social Process and Cultural Theory.* London: Sage.

Featherstone, M. (1991b) *Consumer Culture and Postmodernism.* London: Sage.

Featherstone, M. (1992) Postmodernism and the aestheticization of everyday life, in S. Lash and J. Friedman (eds) *Modernity and Identity.* Oxford: Blackwell.

Featherstone, M. (1995) *Undoing Culture. Globalization, Postmodernism and Identity.* London: Sage.

Featherstone, M. and Hepworth, M. (1985) The history of the male menopause 1848–1936, *Maturitas,* 7: 249–57.

Featherstone, M. and Hepworth, M. (1989) Ageing and old age: Reflections on the postmodern life course, in B. Bytheway, T. Keil, P. Allatt and A. Bryman (eds) *Becoming and Being Old: Sociological Approaches to Later Life.* London: Sage.

Featherstone, M. and Hepworth, M. (1991) The mask of ageing and the postmodern life course, in M. Featherstone, M. Hepworth and B.S. Turner (eds) *The Body: Social Process and Cultural Theory.* London: Sage.

Featherstone, M. and Wernick, A. (eds) (1995) *Images of Aging: Cultural Representations of Later Life.* London: Routledge.

Feher, M., Naddaff, R. and Tazi, N. (1989) *Fragments for a History of the Human Body, Part One.* New York: Zone Books.

Filby, M.P. (1992) 'The figures, the personality and the bums': Service work and sexuality, *Work, Employment and Society,* 6: 23–42.

Finkelstein, V. (1980) *Attitudes and Disabled People: Issues for Discussion.* New York: World Rehabilitation Fund.

Foucault, M. (1963) *Naissance de la Clinique.* Paris: Quadrige/PUF.

Foucault, M. (1971) Nietzsche, geneology, history, in D. Bouchard (ed.) *Language, Counter Memory and Practice.* Oxford: Blackwell.

Foucault, M. (1976a) *Histoire de la Sexualité, Vol. I: La Volonté de Savoir.* Paris: Gallimard.

Foucault, M. (1976b) *The Birth of the Clinic: An Archaeology of Medical Perception.* London: Routledge.

Foucault, M. (1977) *Discipline and Punish: The Birth of the Prison.* Harmondsworth: Penguin (trans. A. Sheridan).

Foucault, M. (1978) *The History of Sexuality, Vol. I: An Introduction.* Harmondsworth: Penguin (trans. R. Hurley).

Foucault, M. (1979) Governmentality, *Ideology and Consciousness*, 6: 5–21.

Foucault, M. (1980) The eye of power, in C. Gordon (ed.) *Power/Knowledge: Michel Foucault, Selected Interviews and Other Writings.* New York: Pantheon Books.

Foucault, M. (1984) *Histoire de la Sexualité, Vol. III: Le Souci de Soi.* Paris: Gallimard.

Foucault, M. (1985) *The History of Sexuality, Vol. II: The Use of Pleasure.* Harmondsworth: Penguin (trans. R. Hurley).

Foucault, M. (1986) *The History of Sexuality, Vol. III: The Care of the Self.* Harmondsworth: Penguin (trans. R. Hurley).

Foucault, M. (1994) L'éthique du souci de soi comme pratique de la liberté, in *Dits et Ecrits, Vol. IV.* Paris: Gallimard.

Foucault, M. (1997) *Ethics: Subjectivity and Truth.* London: Allen Lane (ed. P. Rabinow, trans. R. Hurley).

Fox, N. (1993) *Postmodernism, Sociology and Health.* Buckingham: Open University Press.

Frank, A.W. (1990) Bringing bodies back in: A decade review, *Theory, Culture and Society*, 7(1): 131–62.

Frank, A.W. (1991) For a sociology of the body: An analytical review, in M. Featherstone, M. Hepworth and B.S. Turner (eds) *The Body: Social Process and Cultural Theory.* London: Sage.

Gabe, J., Kelleher, D. and Williams, G. (1994) *Challenging Medicine.* London: Sage.

Gagliardi, A. (1996) Exploring the aesthetic side of organizational life, in S. Clegg, C. Hardy and W. Nord (eds) *Handbook of Organization Studies.* London: Sage.

Gallacher, C. and Laqueur, T. (eds) (1987) *The Making of the Modern Body.* Berkeley, CA: University of California Press.

Giddens, A. (1991) *Modernity and Self Identity: Self and Society in the Late Modern Age.* Cambridge: Polity Press.

Giddens, A. (1992) *The Transformation of Intimacy: Love, Sexuality and Eroticism in Modern Societies.* Cambridge: Polity Press.

Gilbreth, F.B. and Gilbreth, L. (1916) *Fatigue Study.* New York: Stugis and Walton.

Gillon, R. (ed.) (1994) *Principles of Health Care Ethics.* Chichester: John Wiley.

Gilroy, P. (1993) *The Black Atlantic: Modernity and Double Consciousness.* London: Verso.

Glassner, B. (1989) Fitness and the postmodern self, *Journal of Health and Social Behaviour*, 30(June): 180–91.

Glassner, B. (1992) *Bodies: The Tyranny of Perfection.* New York: Lowell House.

Goffman, E. (1968) *Asylums.* Harmondsworth: Penguin.

Goffman, E. (1971a) *Stigma.* Harmondsworth: Penguin.

Goffman, E. (1971b) *The Presentation of Self in Everyday Life.* Harmondsworth: Penguin.

Goldman, P. and Van Houten, D.R. (1980) Bureaucracy and domination: Managerial strategy in turn-of-the-century America, in D. Dunkerley and G. Salaman (eds) *The International Yearbook of Organization Studies 1979.* London: Routledge.

Gouldner, A. (1971) *The Coming Crisis of Western Sociology.* New York: Basic Books.

Green, B.S. (1993) *Gerontology and the Construction of Old Age: A Study in Discourse Analysis*. New York: Aldine de Gruyter.

Greer, G. (1991) *The Change: Women, Ageing and the Menopause*. London: Penguin.

Grosz, E. (1994) *Volatile Bodies: Toward a Corporeal Feminism*. London: Routledge.

Gubrium, J.F. and Wallace, B.J. (1990) Who theorises age?, *Ageing and Society*, 10: 131–49.

Gullette, M.M. (1997) *Declining to Decline: Cultural Combat and the Politics of the Midlife*. Charlottesville, VA: University Press of Virginia.

Hall, E.J. (1993) Waitering/waitressing: Engendering the work of table servers, *Gender and Society*, 17: 329–46.

Hancock, P. and Tyler, M. (2000) 'The look of love': Gender, work and the organization of aesthetics, in J. Hassard, R. Holliday and H. Willmott (eds) *Body and Organization*. London: Sage.

Hand, S. (ed.) (1989) *The Levinas Reader*. Oxford: Blackwell.

Haraway, D. (1990) A manifesto for cyborgs: Science, technology and socialist feminism in the 1980s, reprinted in L. Nicholson (ed.) *Feminism/Postmodernism*. London: Routledge.

Haraway, D. (1991) *Simians, Cyborgs and Women: The Reinvention of Nature*. London: Free Association Books.

Harper, S. (1997) Constructing later life/constructing the body: Some thoughts from feminist theory, in A. Jamieson, S. Harper and C.R. Victor (eds) *Critical Approaches to Ageing and Later Life*. Buckingham: Open University Press.

Hartmann, H. (1979) Capitalism, patriarchy and job segregation by sex, in Z.R. Eisenstein (ed.) *Capitalist Patriarchy and the Case for Socialist Feminism*. New York: Monthly Review Press.

Hasler, F. (1993) Developments in the disabled people's movement, in J. Swain, V. Finkelstein, S. French and M. Oliver (eds) *Disabling Barriers – Enabling Environments*. London: Sage.

Hassard, J. and Holliday, R. (eds) (1998) *Organization Representation*. London: Sage.

Hassard, J., Holliday, R. and Willmott, H. (eds) (2000) *Body and Organization*. London: Sage.

Hazan, H. (1986) Body image and temporality among the aged: A case study of an ambivalent symbol, *Studies in Symbolic Interaction*, 7(A): 305–29.

Hazan, H. and Raz, A.E. (1997) The authorized self: How middle age defines old age in the postmodern, *Semiotica*, 113(3–4): 257–76.

Hearn, J. and Parkin, W. (1995) *'Sex' at 'Work'*, 2nd edn. Brighton: Harvester Wheatsheaf.

Hepworth, M. (1995) Positive ageing: What is the message?, in R. Bunton, S. Nettleton and R. Burrows (eds) *The Sociology of Health Promotion: Critical Analysis of Consumption, Lifestyle and Risk*. London: Routledge.

Hepworth, M. (1999) Review article: In defiance of an ageing culture, *Ageing and Society*, 19: 139–48.

Hepworth, M. and Featherstone, M. (1998) The male menopause: Lay accounts and the cultural reconstruction of midlife, in S. Nettleton and J. Watson (eds) *The Body in Everyday Life*. London: Routledge.

Herzberg, F. (1968) *Work and the Nature of Man*. London: Staples Press.

Hevey, D. (1992) *The Creatures Time Forgot: Photography and Disability Imagery*. London: Routledge.

Hochschild, A.R. (1983) *The Managed Heart*. Berkeley, CA: University of California Press.

Hollway, W. (1984) 'Fitting work': Psychological assessment in organizations, in J. Henriques, W. Hollway, C. Urwin, C. Venn and V. Walkerdine (eds) *Changing the Subject*. New York: Methuen.

Hopper, T. and Macintosh, N. (1998) Management accounting numbers: Freedom or prison – Green versus Foucault, in A. McKinlay and K. Starkey (eds) *Foucault, Management and Organization Theory*. London: Sage.

Horkheimer, M. and Adorno, T. (1973) *The Dialectic of Enlightenment*. London: Allen Lane.

Hughes, B. (1996) Three dimensional man: The new subject of health care expertise, *Caledonian Papers in Social Science*. Department of Social Sciences, Glasgow Caledonian University.

Hughes, B. (1999) The constitution of impairment: Modernity and the aesthetic of oppression, *Disability and Society*, 14(5): 597–610.

Hughes, B. and Paterson, K. (1997) The social model of disability and the disappearing body: Towards a sociology of impairment, *Disability and Society*, 12(3): 325–40.

Hunt, P. (ed.) (1966) *Stigma: The Experience of Disability*. London: Geoffrey Chapman.

Illich, I. (1977) *Disabling Professions*. London: Marion Boyers.

Ingstad, B. and Whyte, S. (eds) (1995) *Disability and Culture*. Berkeley, CA: University of California Press.

Irigaray, L. (1985) *This Sex Which Is Not One*. New York: Cornell University Press (trans. C. Porter).

Irigaray, L. (1993) *An Ethics of Sexual Difference*. London: The Athlone Press (trans. C. Burke and G.C. Gill).

James, N. (1989) Emotional labour: Skill and work in the social regulation of feelings, *Sociological Review*, 37: 15–42.

Jameson, F. (1985) Post-modernism and consumer society, in H. Foster (ed.) *Post-modern Culture*. London: Pluto Press.

Jay, M. (1994) *Downcast Eyes: The Denigration of Vision in Twentieth-Century French Thought*. London: University of California Press.

Jewson, N. (1976) The disappearance of the sick man from medical cosmology, *Sociology*, 10: 225–44.

Johnson, J. and Bytheway, B. (1997) Illustrating care: Images of care relationships with older people, in A. Jamieson, S. Harper and C.R. Victor (eds) *Critical Approaches to Ageing and Later Life*. Buckingham: Open University Press.

Johnston, L. (1996) Flexing femininity: Female body-builders refiguring 'the body', *Gender, Place and Culture*, 3(3): 327–40.

Katz, S. (1992) Alarmist demography: Power, knowledge and the elderly population, *Journal of Aging Studies*, 6(3): 203–25.

Katz, S. (1996) *Disciplining Old Age: The Formation of Gerontological Knowledge*. Charlottesville, VA: University of Virginia Press.

Katz, S. (1997) Foucault and gerontological knowledge: The making of the aged body, in C. O'Farrell (ed.) *Foucault: The Legacy*. Kelvin Grove, Qld: Queensland University of Technology.

Kellner, D. (1995) *Media Culture*. London: Routledge.

Kilbourne, J. (1995) Beauty and the beast of advertising, in G. Dines and J.M. Humez (eds) *Gender, Race and Class in Media*. London: Sage.

Klein, R. (1989) *The Politics of the National Health Service*, 2nd edn. Harlow: Longman.

Kontas, P.C. (1998) Resisting institutionalization: Constructing old age and negotiating home, *Journal of Aging Studies*, 12(2): 167–84.

Kroc, R. (1977) *Grinding It Out: The Making of McDonald's*. New York: St Martin's Press.

Kuhn, A. (1988) The body and cinema: Some problems for feminism, in S. Sheridan (ed.) *Grafts: Essays in Feminist Cultural Theory*. London: Verso.

Laqueur, T. (1990) *Making Sex: Body and Gender from the Greeks to Freud.* Cambridge, MA: Harvard University Press.

Lasch, C. (1980) *The Culture of Narcissism.* New York: Abacus.

Lash, S. (1996) Introduction to the Ethics and Difference Debate, *Theory, Culture and Society,* 13(2): 75–7.

Law, J. and Hassard, J. (eds) (1999) *Actor Network Theory and After.* Oxford: Blackwell and Sociological Review.

Laz, C. (1998) Act your age, *Sociological Forum,* 13(1): 85–113.

Leder, D. (1990) *The Absent Body.* Chicago: Chicago University Press.

Leder, D. (1992) *The Body in Medical Thought and Practice.* Chicago, IL: Chicago University Press.

Leidner, R. (1993) *Fast Food, Fast Talk.* Berkeley, CA: University of California Press.

Lemert, C. (1995) *Sociology after the Crisis.* New York: HarperCollins.

Levin, D. (1988) *The Opening of Vision: Nihilism and the Postmodern Situation.* New York: New York University Press.

Levinas, E. (1981) *Otherwise than Being, or, Beyond Essence.* London: Nijhoff (trans. A. Lingis).

Lipovetsky, G. (1994) *The Empire of Fashion: Dressing Modern Democracy.* Princeton, NJ: Princeton University Press (trans. C. Porter).

Lloyd, M. (1999) The body, in F. Ashe, A. Finlayson, M. Lloyd *et al.* (eds) *Contemporary Social and Political Theory.* Milton Keynes: Open University Press.

Lunt, P. and Livingstone, S. (1992) *Mass Consumption and Personal Identity: Everyday Economic Experience.* Buckingham and Bristol: Open University Press.

Lupton, D. (1994) *Medicine as Culture: Illness, Disease and the Body in Western Societies.* London: Sage.

Lupton, D. (1995) *The Imperative of Health. Public Health and the Regulated Body.* London: Sage.

Lury, C. (1996) *Consumer Culture.* Cambridge: Polity Press.

Lury, C. (1997) *Trying it on.* London: Routledge.

Lynott, R.J. and Lynott, P.P. (1996) Tracing the course of theoretical development in the sociology of ageing, *The Gerontologist,* 36(6): 749–60.

Lyon, D. (1994) *Postmodernity.* Buckingham: Open University Press.

Lyotard, J-F. (1984) *The Postmodern Condition.* Manchester: Manchester University Press.

Lyotard, J-F. (1991) *The Inhuman: Reflections on Time.* Oxford: Polity Press (trans. G. Bennington and R. Bowlby).

Mackay, H. (ed.) (1997) *Consumption and Everyday Life.* Buckingham: Open University Press.

Maffesoli, M. (1996) *The Time of the Tribes.* London: Sage.

Mansfield, A. and McGinn, B. (1993) Pumping irony: The muscular and the feminine, in S. Scott and D. Morgan (eds) *Body Matters.* London: Falmer Press.

Martin, E. (1989) *The Woman in the Body.* Buckingham: Open University Press.

Martin, E. (1994) *Flexible Bodies.* Boston, MA: Beacon Press.

Marx, K. (1990) *Capital: A Critique of Political Economy, Vol. 1.* London: Penguin (first published in 1867).

Maslow, A.H. (1958) *Motivation and Personality.* New York: Harper and Row.

Mayo, E. (1933) *The Human Problems of an Industrial Civilization.* New York: Macmillan.

McKendrick, N., Brew, J. and Plumb, J.H. (1982) *The Birth of Consumer Society.* London: Europa.

McKeown, T. (1976) *The Role of Medicine: Dream, Mirage or Nemesis.* London: Nuffield Provincial Hospital Trust.

McKinlay, A. and Starkey, K. (eds) (1997) *Foucault, Management and Organization Theory*. London: Sage.

McNay, L. (1992) *Foucault and Feminism*. Cambridge: Polity Press.

McRobbie, A. (1994a) Feminism, postmodernism and the real me, in M. Perryman (ed.) *Altered States: Postmodernism, Politics and Culture*. London: Lawrence & Wishart.

McRobbie, A. (1994b) *Postmodernism and Popular Culture*. London: Routledge.

McRobbie, A. (1996) More! New sexualities in girls' and women's magazines, in J. Curran, D. Morley and V. Walkerdine (eds) *Cultural Studies and Communications*. London: Arnold.

Mellor, P. and Shilling, C. (1997) *Re-forming the Body. Religion, Community and Modernity*. London: Sage.

Merleau-Ponty, M. (1945) *Phénomenologie de la Perception*. Paris: Tel Gallimard.

Merleau-Ponty, M. (1962) *The Phenomenology of Perception*. London: Routledge and Kegan Paul (trans. C. Smith).

Merquior, J. (1985) *Foucault*. London: Fontana.

Miller, D., Jackson, P., Thrift, N., Holbrook, B. and Rowlands, M. (1998) *Shopping, Place and Identity*. London: Routledge.

Miller, M. (1981) *The Bon Marché: Bourgeois Culture and the Department Store, 1869–1920*. London: Allen & Unwin.

Mills, C.W. (1967) *The Sociological Imagination*. New York: Oxford University Press (first published 1959).

Mishler, E., Amarasingham, L., Osherson, S. *et al.* (1981) *Social Contexts of Health, Illness and Patient Care*. Cambridge: Cambridge University Press.

Morris, J. (1991) *Pride against Prejudice: Transforming Attitudes to Disability*. London: The Women's Press.

Morris, J. (ed.) (1996) *Encounters with Strangers: Feminism and Disability*. London: The Women's Press.

Myers, K. (1986) *Understains: The Sense and Seduction of Advertising*. London: Pandora.

Nettleton, S. (1995) *The Sociology of Health and Illness*. Cambridge: Polity Press.

Nettleton, S. and Burrows, R. (1994) From bodies in hospitals to people in communities, *Care in Place*, 1(2): 3–13.

Nettleton, S. and Watson, J. (1998) *The Body in Everyday Life*. London: Routledge.

Nicholson, L. and Seidman, S. (eds) (1995) *Social Postmodernism: Beyond Identity Politics*. Cambridge: Cambridge University Press.

Noon, M. and Blyton, P. (1997) *The Realities of Work*. London: Macmillan.

Norton, S. (1996) Jobs, gender and foetal protection policies, *Gender, Work and Organization*, 3(1): 1–12.

Öberg, P. (1996) The absent body: A social gerontological paradox, *Ageing and Society*, 16: 701–19.

Öberg, P. and Tornstam, L. (1999) Body images of men and women of different ages, *Ageing and Society*, 19: 629–44.

Ogden, J. (1992) *Fat Chance: The Myth of Dieting Explained*. London: Routledge.

Oliver, M. (1983) *Social Work with Disabled People*. London: Macmillan.

Oliver, M. (1990) *The Politics of Disablement*. London: Macmillan.

Oliver, M. (1992) Changing the social relations of research production?, *Disability, Handicap and Society*, 7(2): 101–15.

Oliver, M. (1996a) *Understanding Disability: From Theory to Practice*. London: Macmillan.

Oliver, M. (1996b) A sociology of disability or a disablist sociology, in L. Barton (ed.) *Disability and Society: Emerging Issues and Insights*. Harlow: Longman.

Orbach, S. (1986) *Hunger Strike*. London: Faber and Faber.

Pagel, M. (1988) *On Our Own Behalf: An Introduction to the Self-Organisation of Disabled People.* Manchester: GMCDP Publications.

Parker, M. and Cooper, R. (1998) Cyberorganization: Cinema as nervous system, in J. Hassard and R. Holliday (eds) *Organization-Representation.* London: Sage.

Parsons, T. (1951) *The Social System.* London: Routledge and Kegan Paul.

Partington, A. (1991) Melodrama's gendered audience, in S. Franklin, C. Lury and J. Stacey (eds) *Off-centre: Feminism and Cultural Studies.* London: HarperCollins.

Pateman, C. (1988) *The Sexual Contract.* Cambridge: Polity Press.

Paterson, K. and Hughes, B. (1999) Disability studies and phenomenology: The carnal politics of everyday life, *Disability and Society,* 14(5): 597–610.

Peterson, A. and Bunton, R. (1997) *Foucault, Health and Medicine.* London: Routledge.

Phillipson, C. (1982) *Capitalism and the Construction of Old Age.* London: Macmillan.

Phillipson, C. (1998) *Reconstructing Old Age.* London: Sage.

Pinell, P. (1996) Modern medicine and the civilizing process, *Sociology of Health and Illness,* 18(1): 1–16.

Pointon, A. and Davis, C. (eds) (1997) *Framed: Interrogating Disability in the Media.* London: British Film Institute.

Porter, R. (1990) *English Society in the Eighteenth Century.* Harmondsworth: Penguin.

Prado, C.G. (1995) *Starting with Foucault: An Introduction to Genealogy.* Oxford: Westview.

Pringle, R. (1989) *Secretaries Talk: Sexuality, Power and Work.* London: Verso.

Proust, M. (1996) *Time Regained.* London: Vintage.

Rabine, L. (1994) A woman's two bodies: Fashion magazines, consumerism and feminism, in S. Benstock and S. Ferriss (eds) *On Fashion.* New Brunswick, NJ: Rutgers University Press.

Radner, H. (1995) *Shopping Around: Feminine Culture and the Pursuit of Pleasure.* New York: Routledge.

Rafaeli, A. and Pratt, M. (1993) Tailored meanings: On the meaning and impact of organizational dress, *Academy of Management Review,* 18(1): 32–55.

Rafaeli, A. and Sutton, R. (1987) Expression of emotion as part of the work role, *Academy of Management Review,* 32(2): 245–73.

Ramazanoglu, C. (ed.) (1993) *Up Against Foucault: Explorations of some Tensions Between Foucault and Feminism.* London: Routledge.

Rasmussen, D. (1990) *Universalism Versus Communitarianism.* Contemporary Debates in Ethics. Cambridge, MA: MIT Press.

Roethlisberger, F.J. and Dickson, W.J. (1939) *Management and the Worker.* Cambridge, MA: Harvard University Press.

Rose, N. (1996) Identity, genealogy, history, in S. Hall and P. du Gay (eds) *Questions of Cultural Identity.* London: Sage.

Rose, G. (1997) *Love's Work.* London: Vintage.

Rose, N. (1989) *Governing the Soul: Shaping of the Private Self.* London: Routledge.

Rose, N. (1998) Life, reason and history: Reading Georges Canguilhem today, *Economy and Society,* 27(3): 155–70.

Ryan, J. and Thomas, F. (1980) *The Politics of Mental Handicap.* Harmondsworth: Penguin.

Sabo, D. and Gordon, F. (eds) (1995) *Men's Health and Illness: Gender, Power and the Body.* London: Sage.

Sacks, O. (1985) *The Man Who Mistook His Wife for a Hat.* London: Picador.

Sackville-West, V. (1983) *All Passion Spent.* London: Virago (first published 1931).

Safilios-Rothschild, C. (1970) *The Sociology and Social Psychology of Disability and Rehabilitation.* New York: Random House.

Scambler, G. (1991) *Sociology as Applied to Medicine.* London: Bailliere Tindall.

Schama, S. (1987) *The Embarrassment of Riches.* London: Fontana.

Scott, S. and Morgan, D. (1993) *Body Matters.* London: Falmer Press.

Seidman, S. (1998) *Contested Knowledge. Social Theory in the Postmodern Era,* 2nd edn. Oxford: Blackwell.

Sewell, G. and Wilkinson, B. (1992) 'Someone to Watch Over Me': Surveillance, discipline and the just-in-time labour process, *Sociology,* 26(2): 271–89.

Seymour, W. (1998) *Remaking the Body. Rehabilitation and Change.* London: Routledge.

Shakespeare, T. (1992) A response to Liz Crow, *Coalition,* September: 40–2.

Shakespeare, T. (1994) Cultural representations of disabled people: Dustbins for disavowal?, *Disability and Society,* 9(3): 283–301.

Shakespeare, T. (ed.) (1998) *The Disability Reader: Social Science Perspectives.* London: Cassell.

Shakespeare, T. and Watson, N. (1995a) Habemus corpus: Sociology of the body and the issue of impairment. Paper presented at the Quincentennial Conference on the History of Medicine, Aberdeen, 14–16 April.

Shakespeare, T. and Watson, N. (1995b) The Body Line Controversy: A new direction for disability studies? Paper presented at the University of Hull Disability Studies Seminar Series, Hull, 8–10 June.

Shakespeare, T. and Watson, N. (1997) Defending the social model, *Disability and Society,* 12(2): 293–300.

Shildrick, M. (1997) *Leaky Bodies and Boundaries: Feminism, Postmodernism and (Bio)Ethics.* London: Routledge.

Shilling, C. (1993) *The Body and Social Theory.* London: Sage.

Shilling, C. (1997) The body and difference, in K. Woodward (ed.) *Identity and Difference.* London: Sage.

Smart, B. (1996) Facing the body – Goffman, Levinas and the subject of ethics, *Body and Society,* 2(2): 67–98.

Smith, D. (1990) *Texts, Facts and Femininity: Exploring the Relations of Ruling.* London: Routledge.

Stacey, M. (1994) The power of lay knowledge, in J. Popay and G. Williams (eds) *Researching People's Health.* London: Routledge.

Steinberg, D.L. (1997) *Bodies in Glass: Genetics, Eugenics and Embryo Ethics.* Manchester: Manchester University Press.

Steingard, D.S. and Fitzgibbons, D.E. (1993) A postmodern deconstruction of total quality management (TQM), *Journal of Organizational Change Management,* 6(5): 27–42.

Stone, S. (1995) The myth of bodily perfection, *Disability and Society,* 10(4): 413–24.

Strauss, A., Fagerhaugh, B., Suczec, C. and Wiener, C. (1985) *Social Organization of Medical Work.* Chicago, IL: University of Chicago Press.

Susman, R. (1982) *Culture and Commitment 1929–1945.* New York: Braziller.

Swain, J., Finkelstein, V., French, S. and Oliver, M. (eds) (1993) *Disabling Barriers – Enabling Environments.* London: Sage.

Synnott, A. (1993) *The Body Social: Symbolism, Self and Society.* London: Routledge.

Taylor, F.W. (1911) *Principles of Scientific Management.* New York: Harper and Row.

Taylor, P. and Bain, P. (1998) An assembly line in the head: The call centre labour process. Paper presented at the 16th Annual International Labour Process Conference, Manchester, UK, 7–9 April.

Thompson, P. (1992) 'I don't feel old': Subjective ageing and the search for meaning in later life, *Ageing and Society*, 12: 23–47.

Tomlinson, A. (ed.) (1990) *Consumption, Identity and Style: Marketing, Meanings and the Packaging of Pleasure*. London: Routledge.

Townley, B. (1994) *Reframing Human Resource Management*. London: Sage.

Tulle-Winton, E. (1999) Growing old and resistance: Towards a new cultural economy of old age?, *Ageing and Society*, 19: 281–99.

Tulle-Winton, E. and Mooney, E. (1998) The government of old age: Can Foucault help us theorise old age? Paper presented at the XIVth International Sociological Association Congress, Montreal, Canada, July.

Turner, B.S. (1991) Recent developments in the theory of the body, in M. Featherstone, M. Hepworth and B.S. Turner (eds) *The Body. Social Process and Cultural Theory*. London: Sage.

Turner, B.S. (1992) *Regulating Bodies: Essays in Medical Sociology*. London: Routledge.

Turner, B.S. (1994) Introduction, in C. Buci-Glucksmann (1994) *Baroque Reason: The Aesthetics of Modernity*. London: Sage.

Turner, B.S. with Sampson, C. (1995) *Medical Power and Social Knowledge*. London: Sage.

Turner, B.S. (1996) *The Body and Society: Explorations in Social Theory*, 2nd edn. London: Sage.

Turner, T. (1994) Bodies and antibodies: Flesh and fetish in contemporary social theory, in T. Csordas (ed.) *Embodiment and Experience: The Existential Ground of Culture and Self*. Cambridge: Cambridge University Press.

Tyler, M. and Abbott, P. (1998) Chocs away: Weight watching in the contemporary airline industry, *Sociology*, 32(3): 433–50.

UPIAS (Union of Physically Impaired Against Segregation) (1976) *The Fundamental Principles of Disability*. London: Union of Physically Impaired Against Segregation.

Van Maanen, J. (1991) The smile factory: Work at Disneyland, in P. Frost, L. Moore, M.R. Louis, C.C. Lundberg and J. Martin (eds) *Reframing Organizational Culture*. Newbury Park, CA: Sage.

Vattimo, G. (1992) *The End of Modernity*. Cambridge: Polity Press.

Vertinsky, P. (1998) Run, Jane, run: Tensions in the current debate about enhancing women's health through exercise, *Women and Health*, 27(4): 81–111.

Wacquant, L. (1993) Pugs at work: Bodily capital and bodily labour among professional boxers, *Body and Society*, 1(1): 65–93.

Walby, S. (1990) *Theorizing Patriarchy*. Oxford: Blackwell.

Walker, A. (1981) Towards a political economy of old age, *Ageing and Society*, 1: 73–94.

Watson, N. (1998) Enabling identity: Disability, self and citizenship, in T. Shakespeare (ed.) *The Disability Reader: Social Science Perspectives*. London: Cassell.

Weber, M. (1968) *Economy and Society*. Berkeley, CA: University of California Press (first published 1921).

Weiss, M. (1998) Narratives of embodiment: The discursive formulation of multiple bodies, *Semiotica*, 118(3/4): 239–60.

Welsch, W. (1996) Aestheticization processes: Phenomena, distinctions, prospects, *Theory, Culture and Society*, 13(1): 1–24.

Welsch, W. (1997) *Undoing Aesthetics*. London: Sage.

Wendell, S. (1996) *The Rejected Body: Feminist Philosophical Reflections on Disability*. London: Routledge.

Williams, R.H. (1982) *Dream Worlds: Mass Consumption in Late Nineteenth Century France*. Berkeley, CA: University of California Press.

Williams, S. (1998) Health as moral performance: Ritual, transgression and taboo, *Health*, 2(4): 435–57.

Williams, S.J. and Bendelow, G.A. (1998a) Malignant bodies: Children's beliefs about health, cancer and risk, in S. Nettleton and J. Watson (eds) *The Body in Everyday Life*. London: Routledge.

Williams, S.J. and Bendelow, G.A. (1998b) *The Lived Body. Sociological Themes, Embodied Issues*. London: Routledge.

Williams, S. and Calnan, M. (1996) *Modern Medicine: Lay Perspectives and Experiences*. London: UCL Press.

Wilson, E. and Ash, J. (eds) (1992) *Chic Thrills*. Berkeley, CA: University of California Press.

Winship, J. (1983) *Options* – for the way you want to live now, or a magazine for Superwoman, *Theory, Culture and Society*, 1(3): 44–65.

Wolf, N. (1990) *The Beauty Myth*. London: Vintage.

Wolff, K.H. (ed.) (1964) *The Sociology of Georg Simmel*. New York: Free Press.

Woodward, K. (1991) *Aging and its Discontents: Freud and other Fictions*. Bloomington and Indianapolis, IN: Indiana University Press.

Woodward, K. (ed.) (1997) *Identity and Difference*. London: Sage, in association with The Open University.

Woodward, K. (1999) *Figuring Age: Women, Bodies, Generations*. Bloomington, IA: Indiana University Press.

Wray-Bliss, E. and Parker, M. (1998) Marxism, capitalism and ethics, in M. Parker (ed.) *Ethics and Organizations*. London: Sage.

Zarb, G. (1992) On the road to Damascus: First steps towards changing the relations of disability research production, *Disability, Handicap and Society*, 7(2): 125–38.

Zola, I. (1972) Medicine as an institution of social control, *Sociological Review*, 20: 487–503.

Zuboff, S. (1988) *In the Age of the Smart Machine*. London: Heinemann.

Index

MALE BODIES
HEALTH, CULTURE AND IDENTITY

Jonathan Watson

> This is an important and timely book which draws recent theorizing about the body into the frame of everyday experience in a manner relevant to the practical concerns of health promotion . . . skilfully explores lay accounts about health and interprets them in terms of different concepts of embodiment.
>
> Professor Gareth Williams, School of Social Sciences,
> Cardiff University

- How do men perceive their bodies?
- How can empirical study of the body inform our understanding of the social world of men?
- What are the implications for public health?

These days it seems that everyone has a view on what it means to be 'a man' and why men behave in the way they do. The irony is that very little of this debate is informed by what men themselves have to say. This lively and engaging book takes an in-depth look at three key contemporary issues – health, identity and the body – by exploring how 'ordinary' men talk about their bodies and experience them in a variety of circumstances. Designed to complement the considerable theoretical work on the body over the past decade, *Male Bodies* draws on qualitative and quantitative data as well as addressing theoretical issues. It demonstrates the importance of developing an empirically and theoretically informed approach to men's health based on an understanding of male embodiment. It will be invaluable to students and researchers in sociology, health, gender and cultural studies, as well as health professionals concerned with men's health.

Contents
Introduction – Dominant perspectives shaping men's health – Social theory, the body and health – The contribution of lay knowledge – The male body in everyday life – The idea of embodiment – Prevention and agency – Men's health: some conclusions – Appendix: biographical profiles – Bibliography – Index.

176pp   0 335 19785 X (Paperback)   0 335 19786 8 (Hardback)